Total
Palmistry

Total Palmistry

the love connection

Rafe Anderson

Red Wheel
Boston, MA / York Beach, ME

First published in 2003 by
Red Wheel/Weiser, LLC
York Beach, ME 03910
With offices at:
368 Congress Street
Boston, MA 02210
www.redwheelweiser.com

ISBN: 1-59003-028-1

Typeset in Kennerly

Printed in Canada

TCP

10 09 08 07 06 05 04 03
 8 7 6 5 4 3 2 1

What is *Total Palmistry*?

Unlike most palmistry books that cover general palm reading topics in tire-some detail, *Total Palmistry* is all about how your palm reflects your love life. Rather than bore you with interpretations that don't apply to your specific hand, this book gives you what you desire—your own personal love reading! That's right, the unique format makes it possible for you to read your palm, or your lover's palm, in just minutes. Your experiences will be unique and your readings will be personal!

What you should know

It's important to understand that Palmistry is one of the oldest methodolo-gies known to humankind. This incredible form of self-exploration is intended to provide you with an opportunity to leverage your strengths as well as improve upon any potential weaknesses.

Keep in mind that your palm does not control your fate, but rather your palm is a reflection of your approach to life and your ability to handle some of life's most significant challenges.

How to use this book

While everyone's love reading begins with the same question, the romantic path you take through this book is as unique as your hand.

So examine your hand, or your lover's hand, and answer every question to the best of your ability. Once you have chosen your answer, go to the assigned page for that answer. Continue on from there in the same way until your reading is finally complete. It's that simple. Let's get started!

Starting with the mounts

"The hand reflects all the changes of the brain, and the subject will belong to the type as shown by the best-marked Mount in the hand."

-William Benham, "The Father of Modern Palmistry"

Your palm is naturally divided into seven mounts. One of the most important tasks when reading a palm is determining which mount is most prominent. Each mount reflects an influence on your character. Just as an inflated mount may represent a strong influence, a deflated mount can reflect a lack in character traits represented by the mount in question. Let's start your reading by examining your mounts.

Which mount on your hand is most prominent?

INSTRUCTIONS: Completely relax and cup your palm in front of you. Closely examine your hand in a well-lit area and look to see which mount is most dominant. Be sure to use the hand you write with.

HINT: Don't assume that it's "mount g." The most prominent mount will stand out on your hand like a mountain.

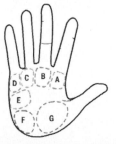

A. mount a (go to page 4)
B. mount b (go to page 5)
C. mount c (go to page 6)
D. mount d (go to page 7)
E. mount e (go to page 8)
F. mount f (go to page 9)
G. mount g (go to page 10)

You're a Jupiterian – take charge!

Due to your prominent mount of Jupiter you are best characterized as a Jupiterian. It appears that you matured early in life and you are most likely to marry at a young age.

Meanwhile, your pleasant demeanor will have a significant influence on anyone you hold close to your heart.

How much hair do you have on the back of your hands?

INSTRUCTIONS: Take a moment to examine the back of your hand. Using your best judgment determine how much hair you have.

HINT: Don't be fooled by the color of the hair. Blond hair may be more difficult to see, but that doesn't mean there's less of it.

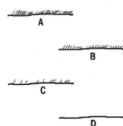

A. lots of hair (go to page 11)
B. moderate amount (go to page 12)
C. hardly any (go to page 13)
D. none at all (go to page 14)

You're a Saturnian!

Based on your examination of your hand's mounts it appears that you are what's known as a Saturnian. Your wise nature helps guide you into relationships that are truly rewarding. The fact is you always think before you act.

While you have some strong relationships you do not fear solitude. This means that you are less likely to marry early in life. Don't let others rush you into anything that you're not ready for.

What is the general shape of your fingertips?

INSTRUCTIONS: Take a close look at your fingers and determine the general shape of your fingertips. Compare your fingertips to the images to the left.

HINT: Try holding your fingertips up to the light and viewing their silhouettes.

A. spatulate (go to page 27)
B. square (go to page 28)
C. conic (go to page 29)
D. pointed (go to page 30)

You're an Apollonian!

As an Apollonian, you are healthy, vigorous, attractive, and a lover of beauty. You live for independence and the opportunity to date and meet many new people.

As an Apollonian, you are likely to enjoy life to its fullest and therefore bring joy to those around you. It's interesting to see that you have a tendency to surround yourself with people and things that are physically attractive.

How much hair do you have on the back of your hands?

INSTRUCTIONS: Take a moment to examine the back of your hand. Using your best judgment determine how much hair you have.

HINT: Don't be fooled by the color of the hair. Blond hair may be more difficult to see, but that doesn't mean there's less of it.

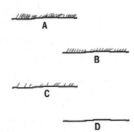

A. lots of hair (go to page 15)
B. moderate amount (go to page 16)
C. hardly any (go to page 17)
D. none at all (go to page 18)

You're a Mercurian!

As a Mercurian you are balanced and even in action. You seek romance more for its comfort than its excitement.

Unfortunately your desire for stability and comfort will cause you to miss out on the thrills that are often associated with feelings of love. Of course stability is important, but be sure you avoid falling into a romantic routine that leaves little opportunity for surprise.

What is the general shape of your fingertips?

INSTRUCTIONS: Take a close look at your fingers and determine the general shape of your fingertips. Compare your fingertips to the images to the left.

HINT: Try holding your fingertips up to the light and viewing their silhouettes.

A

B

A. spatulate (go to page 31)
B. square (go to page 32)
C. conic (go to page 33)
D. pointed (go to page 34)

C

D

Believe it or not—you're a Martian!

As a Martian you will fight unquestionably for your friends and loved ones and spend your money freely with them and on their behalf.

When you fall in love it's with all the intensity of your strong nature, and you storm the heart of the one you admire with vigor and ease. People are usually quite intrigued with your willingness to take risks.

How much hair do you have on the back of your hands?

INSTRUCTIONS: Take a moment to examine the back of your hand. Using your best judgment determine how much hair you have.

HINT: Don't be fooled by the color of the hair. Blond hair may be more difficult to see, but that doesn't mean there's less of it.

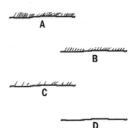

A. lots of hair (go to page 19)
B. moderate amount (go to page 20)
C. hardly any (go to page 21)
D. none at all (go to page 22)

You're a Lunarian!

While you are not as strongly impelled toward matrimony as some of the other types, you don't avoid it entirely.

You are sometimes incapable of strong affection. In most cases you are likely to date and eventually marry someone who is significantly older or younger than you are.

What is the general shape of your fingertips?

INSTRUCTIONS: Take a close look at your fingers and determine the general shape of your fingertips. Compare your fingertips to the images to the left.

HINT: Try holding your fingertips up to the light and viewing their silhouettes.

A. spatulate (go to page 35)
B. square (go to page 36)
C. conic (go to page 37)
D. pointed (go to page 38)

You're a Venusian!

It appears that you are a Venusian. Your strong mount of Venus indicates that you are extremely generous and affectionate. You are attracted to the warmth and love found in fellowship with others.

Your passion is intense and visible to just about everyone. Ultimately, you would put everything on the line for those you love. Be sure you're getting what you deserve in return!

How much hair do you have on the back of your hands?

Instructions: Take a moment to examine the back of your hand. Using your best judgment determine how much hair you have.

HINT: Don't be fooled by the color of the hair. Blond hair may be more difficult to see, but that doesn't mean there's less of it.

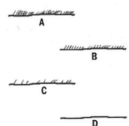

A. lots of hair (go to page 23)
B. moderate amount (go to page 24)
C. hardly any (go to page 25)
D. none at all (go to page 26)

You and your hairy hand

Generally hair on the hand represents significant physical strength. Coupled with this physical strength is determination that's inherent in most Jupiterians.

The fact is you always like to have the last word and you're constantly attempting to prove yourself. While this may cause controversy in your romantic relationships, it may also serve as a positive force as you are willing to struggle tirelessly to better your relationship. Ultimately, your determination can both work for you and against you.

Let's continue your reading. . .

How flexible are your fingers?

INSTRUCTIONS: Use your passive hand to bend back the fingers on your active hand. Determine how flexible your fingers are by examining the angle created by the base of your fingers and the top of your palm.

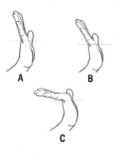

HINT: Be sure you are bending your fingers. Don't make the mistake of bending back your entire hand.

A. minimum flexibility (go to page 39)
B. medium flexibility (go to page 40)
C. maximum flexibility (go to page 41)

The hair on your hand

Your moderately hairy hand represents physical strength and determination. You may have difficulty agreeing with those you hold close to your heart. Perhaps because your hands are extremely hairy, you have a competitive approach to every disagreement.

Fortunately the hair on your hand is not overwhelming. In fact, despite your competitive nature you're committed to working through a relationship's most significant challenges.

Let's continue your reading. . .

Which third of your fingers is longer?

INSTRUCTIONS: Your fingers are naturally split into thirds. Each third is called a phalanx. It's up to you to examine your fingers and determine which phalanx is generally the longest. Are you having fun or what?

HINT: Look at the space between the joints.

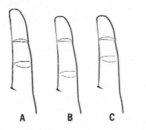

A. the top (go to page 42)
B. the middle (go to page 43)
C. the bottom (go to page 44)

You and your (mostly) hairless hand

Since hair on the hand is believed to be a sign of physical strength, the minimal amount of hair on your hand indicates that you may not command the physical force and determination enjoyed by some of your hairier friends.

In your romantic relationships you are often dominated by your mate, either emotionally or physically, and should beware of situations that may threaten your own well-being.

However, your easygoing nature may also be a positive force in your romantic relationship if you are matched with someone who will not take advantage of your weakness in this area.

Let's continue your reading. . .

How flexible are your fingers?

INSTRUCTIONS: Use your passive hand to bend back the fingers on your active hand. Determine how flexible your fingers are by examining the angle created by the base of your fingers and the top of your palm.

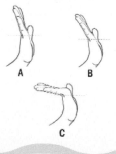

HINT: Be sure you are bending your fingers. Don't make the mistake of bending back your entire hand.

A. minimum flexibility (go to page 39)
B. medium flexibility (go to page 40)
C. maximum flexibility (go to page 41)

You and your hairless hand

Since it's believed that hair represents significant physical strength and determination, your hairless hand indicates that you may need some support.

You need to be careful if you surround yourself with people with hairy hands, and particularly careful if you're dealing with a romantic partner with hands much hairier than your own. If this is the case you will often find yourself being controlled and manipulated. It is important for you to stand your ground and not back down in these situations.

Let's continue your reading. . .

Which third of your fingers is longer?

INSTRUCTIONS: Your fingers are naturally split into thirds. Each third is called a phalanx. It's up to you to examine your fingers and determine which phalanx is generally the longest. Are you having fun or what?

HINT: Look at the space between the joints.

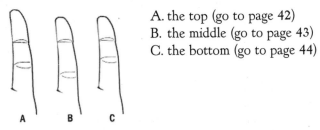

A. the top (go to page 42)
B. the middle (go to page 43)
C. the bottom (go to page 44)

You and your hairy hand

Your hairy hand represents significant physical strength. Typically, the hair of the Apollonian is of a brilliant, golden hue and this contributes to the vigorous constitution you possess. If your hair happens to be black, it adds even more sparkle to your already sparkling character.

Coupled with your physical strength is determination. You always like to have the last word and you're always trying to prove yourself. This may cause controversy in your romantic relationships, but also serves as a positive force as you are willing to struggle tirelessly to better your relationship. Ultimately, your determination can both work for you and against you.

Let's continue your reading. . .

How flexible are your fingers?

INSTRUCTIONS: Use your passive hand to bend back the fingers on your active hand. Determine how flexible your fingers are by examining the angle created by the base of your fingers and the top of your palm.

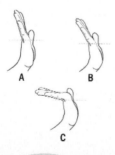

HINT: Be sure you are bending your fingers. Don't make the mistake of bending back your entire hand.

A. minimum flexibility (go to page 45)
B. medium flexibility (go to page 46)
C. maximum flexibility (go to page 47)

The hair on your hand

Your moderately hairy hand represents physical strength and determination. Typically, the hair of the Apollonian is of a brilliant, golden hue and this contributes to the vigorous constitution you possess. If your hair happens to be black, it adds even more sparkle to your already sparkling character.

Additionally, you like to have the last word and you will always look for a way to prove yourself. Perhaps because your hands are moderately hairy, you approach every argument like it's a competition. This may cause friction in your relationships but can also work for you, as your mate appreciates your serious nature and determination.

Let's continue your reading. . .

Which third of your fingers is longer?

INSTRUCTIONS: Your fingers are naturally split into thirds. Each third is called a phalanx. It's up to you to examine your fingers and determine which phalanx is generally the longest. Are you having fun or what?

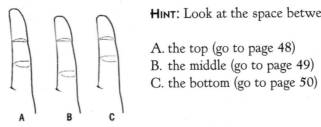

HINT: Look at the space between the joints.

A. the top (go to page 48)
B. the middle (go to page 49)
C. the bottom (go to page 50)

A   B   C

You and your (mostly) hairless hand

Since hair on the hand is believed to be a sign of physical strength, your hand suggests that you may not command the physical force and determination enjoyed by some of your hairier friends.

In your romantic relationships you are often dominated by your mate, either emotionally or physically, and should beware of situations that may threaten your own well-being. However, your easygoing nature may also be a positive force in your romantic relationship if you are matched with someone who will not take advantage of your weakness in this area.

Let's continue your reading. . .

How flexible are your fingers?

INSTRUCTIONS: Use your passive hand to bend back the fingers on your active hand. Determine how flexible your fingers are by examining the angle created by the base of your fingers and the top of your palm.

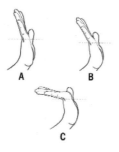

HINT: Be sure you are bending your fingers. Don't make the mistake of bending back your entire hand.

A. minimum flexibility (go to page 45)
B. medium flexibility (go to page 46)
C. maximum flexibility (go to page 47)

You and your hairless hand

Since it's believed that hair represents significant physical strength and determination, your hairless hand indicates that you may not be as physically or emotionally strong as some of your hairy friends.

Time to take notice—you need to be careful if you're surrounding yourself with people with hairy hands. You will often find yourself being controlled and manipulated. It is important for you to stand your ground and not back down in these situations.

Let's continue your reading. . .

Which third of your fingers is longer?

INSTRUCTIONS: Your fingers are naturally split into thirds. Each third is called a phalanx. It's up to you to examine your fingers and determine which phalanx is generally the longest. Are you having fun or what?

HINT: Look at all your fingers. Upon close examination you should be able to determine which section is most substantial.

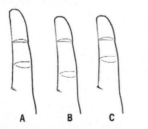

A. the top (go to page 48)
B. the middle (go to page 49)
C. the bottom (go to page 50)

You and your hairy hand

Your hairy hand represents significant physical strength. Since you are a Martian you are already full of vigor and physical strength. Coupled with your physical strength is determination.

You always like to have the last word and you're always trying to prove yourself. This may cause controversy in your romantic relationships, but also serves as a positive force as you are willing to struggle tirelessly to better your relationship. Ultimately, your determination can work both for you and against you.

Let's continue your reading. . .

How flexible are your fingers?

INSTRUCTIONS: Use your passive hand to bend back the fingers on your active hand. Determine how flexible your fingers are by examining the angle created by the base of your fingers and the top of your palm.

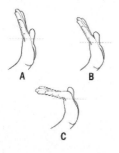

HINT: Be sure you are bending your fingers. Don't make the mistake of bending back your entire hand.

A. minimum flexibility (go to page 51)
B. medium flexibility (go to page 52)
C. maximum flexibility (go to page 53)

The hair on your hand

Your moderately hairy hand represents physical strength and determination. You like to have the last word and you will always look for a way to prove yourself.

Perhaps because your hands are moderately hairy, you approach every argument like it's a competition. While this may cause friction in your relationships it can also work for you, as your mate appreciates your serious nature and determination.

Let's continue your reading. . .

Which third of your fingers is longer?

INSTRUCTIONS: Your fingers are naturally split into thirds. Each third is called a phalanx. It's up to you to examine your fingers and determine which phalanx is generally the longest. Are you having fun or what?

HINT: Look at all your fingers. Upon close examination you should be able to determine which section is most substantial.

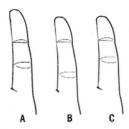

A

B

C

A. the top (go to page 54)
B. the middle (go to page 55)
C. the bottom (go to page 56)

You and your (mostly) hairless hand

Since hair on the hand is believed to be a sign of physical strength, your hand suggests that you may not command the physical force and determination enjoyed by some of your hairier friends.

In your romantic relationships you are often dominated by your mate, either emotionally or physically, and should beware of situations that may threaten your own well-being. However, your easygoing nature may also be a positive force in your romantic relationship if you are matched with someone who will not take advantage of your weakness in this area.

Let's continue your reading. . .

How flexible are your fingers?

INSTRUCTIONS: Use your passive hand to bend back the fingers on your active hand. Determine how flexible your fingers are by examining the angle created by the base of your fingers and the top of your palm.

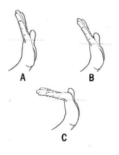

HINT: Be sure you are bending your fingers. Don't make the mistake of bending back your entire hand.

A. minimum flexibility (go to page 51)
B. medium flexibility (go to page 52)
C. maximum flexibility (go to page 53)

You and your hairless hand

Since it's believed that hair represents significant physical strength and determination, your hairless hand indicates that you may not be as physically or emotionally strong as some of your hairy friends.

You need to be careful if you're surrounding yourself with people with hairy hands, and particularly careful if dealing with a romantic partner with hands much hairier than your own. If this is the case you will often find yourself being controlled and manipulated. It is important for you to stand your ground and not back down in these situations.

Let's continue your reading. . .

Which third of your fingers is longer?

INSTRUCTIONS: Your fingers are naturally split into thirds. Each third is called a phalanx. It's up to you to examine your fingers and determine which phalanx is generally the longest. Are you having fun or what?

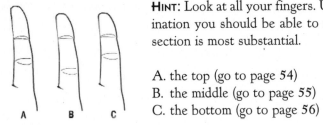

HINT: Look at all your fingers. Upon close examination you should be able to determine which section is most substantial.

A. the top (go to page 54)
B. the middle (go to page 55)
C. the bottom (go to page 56)

You and your hairy hand

Surprisingly, the hair on your hand reveals a tendency to be a bit forceful. However, as a Venusian, you're more likely to handle all conflicts in a loving manner. Your determination will probably have a positive impact on your love life.

Let's continue your reading. . .

How flexible are your fingers?

INSTRUCTIONS: Use your passive hand to bend back the fingers on your active hand. Determine how flexible your fingers are by examining the angle created by the base of your fingers and the top of your palm.

HINT: Be sure you are bending your fingers. Don't make the mistake of bending back your entire hand.

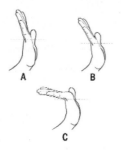

A. minimum flexibility (go to page 57)
B. medium flexibility (go to page 58)
C. maximum flexibility (go to page 59)

The hair on your hand
As we focus on the hair on your hand we see signs of physical strength and determination. Your ability to overpower others is obvious and this will play a significant role in the way you communicate with your lover. While your words may not be offensive, the way you deliver them may be.

Let's continue your reading. . .

Which third of your fingers is longer?
INSTRUCTIONS: Your fingers are naturally split into thirds. Each third is called a phalanx. It's up to you to examine your fingers and determine which phalanx is generally the longest. Are you having fun or what?

HINT: Look at all your fingers. Upon close examination you should be able to determine which section is most substantial.

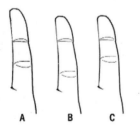

A. the top (go to page 60)
B. the middle (go to page 61)
C. the bottom (go to page 62)

You and your (mostly) hairless hand

It's interesting to discover that hair on your hand suggests that you may not command the physical force and determination enjoyed by some of your hairier friends. You rely on quick wits before brutish force. Your lover will appreciate this.

Moreover, your easygoing nature may also be a positive force in your romantic relationship if you are matched with someone who will not take advantage of your passive approach.

Let's continue your reading. . .

How flexible are your fingers?

INSTRUCTIONS: Use your passive hand to bend back the fingers on your active hand. Determine how flexible your fingers are by examining the angle created by the base of your fingers and the top of your palm.

HINT: Be sure you are bending your fingers. Don't make the mistake of bending back your entire hand.

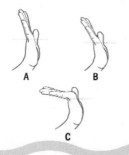

A. minimum flexibility (go to page 57)
B. medium flexibility (go to page 58)
C. maximum flexibility (go to page 59)

You and your hairless hand

Since it's believed that hair represents significant physical strength and determination, your hairless hand indicates that you may not be as physically or emotionally strong as some of your hairy friends.

You need to be careful if you're surrounding yourself with people with hairy hands, and particularly careful if dealing with a romantic partner with hands much hairier than your own. If this is the case you will often find yourself being controlled and manipulated. It is important for you to stand your ground and not back down in these situations.

Let's continue your reading. . .

Which third of your fingers is longer?

INSTRUCTIONS: Your fingers are naturally split into thirds. Each third is called a phalanx. It's up to you to examine your fingers and determine which phalanx is generally the longest. Are you having fun or what?

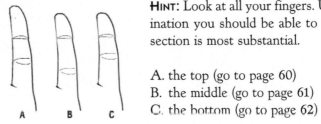

HINT: Look at all your fingers. Upon close examination you should be able to determine which section is most substantial.

A. the top (go to page 60)
B. the middle (go to page 61)
C. the bottom (go to page 62)

Your spatulate tips

Your spatulate fingertips add the spark of activity and originality to your Saturnian wisdom and sobriety. They indicate that you are a great worker in your chosen field and are more likely to socialize than your fellow Saturnians.

However, if your spatulate tips are extremely pronounced you will be harder to get along with, having a gloomy, sullen, and morose personality.

Let's continue your reading. . .

Which third of your fingers is longer?

INSTRUCTIONS: Your fingers are naturally split into thirds. Each third is called a phalanx. It's up to you to examine your fingers and determine which phalanx is generally the longest. Are you having fun or what?

HINT: Look at all your fingers. Upon close examination you should be able to determine which section is most substantial.

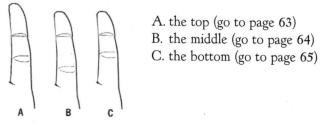

A. the top (go to page 63)
B. the middle (go to page 64)
C. the bottom (go to page 65)

Strictly square

Your square fingertips indicate that you are practical, have a great deal of common sense, and do not believe in superstitions, although this is common among Saturnian types.

Your practicality serves you well in your area of expertise, especially in the realms of farming, chemistry, medicine, physics, or math. Socially, you often become very quiet and sober and even tend toward melancholy.

Let's continue your reading. . .

Which third of your fingers is longer?

INSTRUCTIONS: Your fingers are naturally split into thirds. Each third is called a phalanx. It's up to you to examine your fingers and determine which phalanx is generally the longest. Are you having fun or what?

HINT: Look at all your fingers. Upon close examination you should be able to determine which section is most substantial.

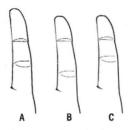

A. the top (go to page 63)
B. the middle (go to page 64)
C. the bottom (go to page 65)

A   B   C

Your conic fingertips

Your conic fingertips, if only present on your Saturn finger, indicate that you have an exaggerated dose of the Saturnian qualities of wisdom, prudence, and gloominess.

If, however, all your fingertips are conic, you are more balanced in character and may prove to be more vibrant and social.

Let's continue your reading. . .

Which third of your fingers is longer?

INSTRUCTIONS: Your fingers are naturally split into thirds. Each third is called a phalanx. It's up to you to examine your fingers and determine which phalanx is generally the longest. Are you having fun or what?

HINT: Look at all your fingers. Upon close examination you should be able to determine which section is most substantial.

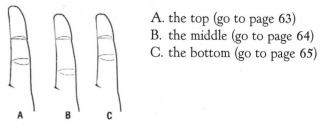

A. the top (go to page 63)
B. the middle (go to page 64)
C. the bottom (go to page 65)

Quite pointed
Your pointed fingertips, on the middle finger in particular, are a sign of excessive idealism. You are ruled by dreams, signs, and omens, and like most Saturnians, you are deeply superstitious. Your character is thus more erratic and less balanced, making you difficult to get along with at times.

Let's continue your reading. . .

Which third of your fingers is longer?

Instructions: Your fingers are naturally split into thirds. Each third is called a phalanx. It's up to you to examine your fingers and determine which phalanx is generally the longest. Are you having fun or what?

Hint: Look at all your fingers. Upon close examination you should be able to determine which section is most substantial.

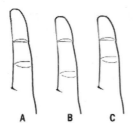

A. the top (go to page 63)
B. the middle (go to page 64)
C. the bottom (go to page 65)

Your spatulate tips

Your spatulate fingertips are a sign that you are active in your search for new discoveries in old sciences. As a Mercurian, you are not satisfied to follow trails that others have made.

Spatulate tips also indicate that you are practical and rely on common sense. You are always on the go, and those who surround you are motivated by your wonderful enthusiasm and activity.

Let's continue your reading. . .

Which third of your fingers is longer?

INSTRUCTIONS: Your fingers are naturally split into thirds. Each third is called a phalanx. It's up to you to examine your fingers and determine which phalanx is generally the longest. Are you having fun or what?

HINT: Look at all your fingers. Upon close examination you should be able to determine which section is most substantial.

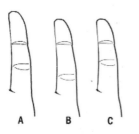

A. the top (go to page 66)
B. the middle (go to page 67)
C. the bottom (go to page 68)

Your square tips

Your square fingertips indicate a strong desire for regularity and organization. Like many Mercurians, you are known for your commonsense approach and place a high value on practicality.

You weigh your decisions carefully and are never rash. Your balanced and steady manner makes you a good mate, but your lack of spontaneity may make your relationships dull.

Let's continue your reading. . .

Where does your heart line end?

INSTRUCTIONS: Your heart line should travel from someplace near your index finger toward the other side of your hand. Heart lines end in different places on everybody's hands.

HINT: Follow your heart line to the end.

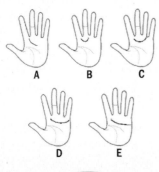

A. middle of the hand (go to page 194)
B. below the middle finger (go to page 195)
C. below the ring finger (go to page 196)
D. below the pinky finger (go to page 197)
E. other side of the palm (go to page 198)

Your conic tips

Your conic fingertips indicate that you are an artistic and intuitive person. Your Mercurian intuition serves you well as you are a quick thinker and an eloquent speaker.

Your fingertips also indicate that you appreciate the beauty in your closest friends. You love all that attracts the eye or pleases the ear, and life seems less a matter of labor than enjoyment for you.

Now let's continue to examine your fingers. . .

Which third of your fingers is longer?

INSTRUCTIONS: Your fingers are naturally split into thirds. Each third is called a phalanx. It's up to you to examine your fingers and determine which phalanx is generally the longest. Are you having fun or what?

HINT: Look at all your fingers. Upon close examination you should be able to determine which section is most substantial.

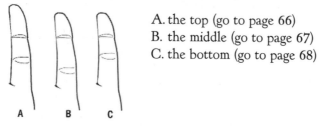

A. the top (go to page 66)
B. the middle (go to page 67)
C. the bottom (go to page 68)

Quite pointed

Your pointed fingertips indicate that you are an idealist. This quality influences all your endeavors, even the typical Mercurian realm of the sciences.

You bring to this discipline, and others, your great imagination and vision. You may struggle if you are in a relationship with someone who is overly practical. Be careful around anyone with square fingertips. You may never be fully understood by those who are most practical.

Let's continue your reading. . .

Where does your heart line end?

INSTRUCTIONS: Your heart line should travel from someplace near your index finger toward the other side of your hand. Heart lines end in different places on everybody's hands.

HINT: Follow your heart line to the end.

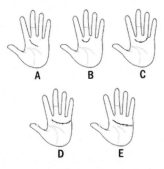

A. middle of the hand (go to page 194)
B. below the middle finger (go to page 195)
C. below the ring finger (go to page 196)
D. below the pinky finger (go to page 197)
E. other side of the palm (go to page 198)

Your spatulate tips

Your spatulate fingertips add an extra dimension of activity to your already restless Lunarian personality. You are original and completely unconventional, sometimes to an overexaggerated degree that causes you trouble.

Occasionally your overactive imagination causes you to become flighty, making you difficult for others to understand and put up with.

Let's continue your reading. . .

Which third of your fingers is longer?

INSTRUCTIONS: Your fingers are naturally split into thirds. Each third is called a phalanx. It's up to you to examine your fingers and determine which phalanx is generally the longest. Are you having fun or what?

HINT: Look at all your fingers. Upon close examination you should be able to determine which section is most substantial.

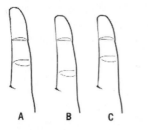

A. the top (go to page 102)
B. the middle (go to page 103)
C. the bottom (go to page 104)

Strictly square

Your square fingertips indicate that you are practical. You have a healthy imagination typical of the Lunarian, but it is well paired with common sense and practical ideas.

This combination brings you success, especially as a composer, historian, or musician. You are regular in your habits and thoughts, making you a constant and reliable companion.

Let's continue your reading. . .

Which third of your fingers is longer?

INSTRUCTIONS: Your fingers are naturally split into thirds. Each third is called a phalanx. It's up to you to examine your fingers and determine which phalanx is generally the longest. Are you having fun or what?

HINT: Look at all your fingers. Upon close examination you should be able to determine which section is most substantial.

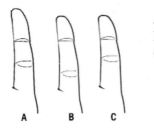

A. the top (go to page 102)
B. the middle (go to page 103)
C. the bottom (go to page 104)

Your conic tips

Your conic fingertips are typical of the Lunarian type and are an indication of finely tuned intuitive qualities.

You are a fanciful, romantic person and tend to be lazy, hating physical and intellectual strain. Your complacency may put strain on both your business and personal relationships.

Let's continue your reading. . .

Which third of your fingers is longer?

INSTRUCTIONS: Your fingers are naturally split into thirds. Each third is called a phalanx. It's up to you to examine your fingers and determine which phalanx is generally the longest. Are you having fun or what?

HINT: Look at all your fingers. Upon close examination you should be able to determine which section is most substantial.

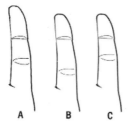

A. the top (go to page 102)
B. the middle (go to page 103)
C. the bottom (go to page 104)

A   B   C

Quite pointed

Your pointed fingertips indicate that you are an idealist. Your interest in religious exaltation, mysticism, and superstition will engage you in impractical pursuits, and some may say you have wasted your life in these endeavors. You will find that many misunderstand your lifestyle.

Let's continue your reading. . .

Which third of your fingers is longer?

INSTRUCTIONS: Your fingers are naturally split into thirds. Each third is called a phalanx. It's up to you to examine your fingers and determine which phalanx is generally the longest. Are you having fun or what?

HINT: Look at all your fingers. Upon close examination you should be able to determine which section is most substantial.

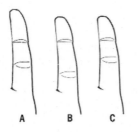

A. the top (go to page 102)
B. the middle (go to page 103)
C. the bottom (go to page 104)

Stiff fingers

Your hand's flexibility is limited, therefore you are cautious, close-minded, and you lack adaptability. In relationships you may be conservative and avoid taking risks, such as making the first move.

You often find yourself intimidated by new ventures and new ideas, and do not wish to venture out of the traditional boundaries established for love and romantic life, choosing a mate who shares your conservative tastes.

Let's continue your reading. . .

Where does your heart line begin?

INSTRUCTIONS: In general your heart line starts on the same side of your hand as your thumb. Select the answer that best describes the starting point of your heart line.

HINT: Hold your hand close to the light.

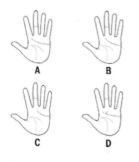

A. below the index finger (go to page 77)
B. between the index finger and middle finger (go to page 78)
C. below the middle finger (go to page 79)
D. branches from both fingers (go to page 80)

A   B

C   D

Now bend a little

You are balanced, even in action, and you have complete control of yourself. As a partner you listen well and understand the concerns of your mate.

Your natural tendency toward balance often finds you in relationships that are highly stable as you strive to avoid the extremes. As a partner you are neither held back by traditional ideas of relationships, nor rashly impelled to become a part of the latest romantic trend.

Let's continue your reading. . .

How flexible is the tip of your thumb?

INSTRUCTIONS: Hold your thumb in the air and bend the tip of your thumb back without any assistance from your other hand.

HINT: You are only determining the flexibility of the tip of your thumb.

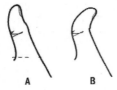

A. stiff (go to page 81)
B. flexible (go to page 82)

Let's get flexible

Your hands are extremely flexible and therefore so are your heart and mind. Ultimately, you are open to new ideas and willing to consider alternative perspectives in the realm of love and relationships.

Your romantic relationships may benefit from your ability to compromise and your overall spontaneity.

Let's continue your reading. . .

Where does your heart line begin?

INSTRUCTIONS: In general your heart line starts on the same side of your hand as your thumb. Select the answer that best describes the starting point of your heart line.

HINT: Hold your hand close to the light.

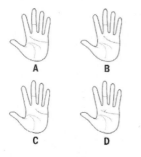

A. below the index finger (go to page 77)
B. between the index finger and middle finger (go to page 78)
C. below the middle finger (go to page 79)
D. branches from both fingers (go to page 80)

Long on top

Close examination of your fingers reveals that you are ruled by your mind. You are absorbed in matters of the mind and you have a desire to be challenged intellectually.

You are uninterested in those who aren't as intellectual as you are and therefore may appear standoffish or snobby to those who don't know you.

Let's continue your reading. . .

How flexible is the tip of your thumb?

INSTRUCTIONS: Hold your thumb in the air and bend the tip of your thumb back without any assistance from your other hand.

HINT: You are only determining the flexibility of the tip of your thumb.

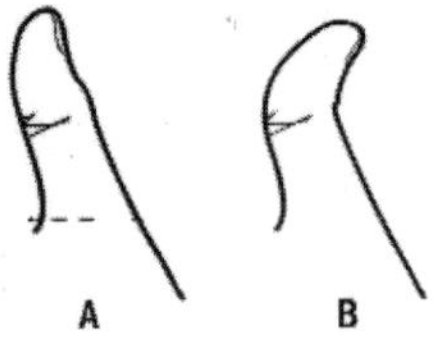

A

B

A. stiff (go to page 81)
B. flexible (go to page 82)

Long in the middle

Close examination of your fingers reveals that you are more interested in making money than finding love. You are consumed with financial success.

You may discover that your satisfaction in a relationship is often determined by your own financial standing, or that of your partner. You may be in danger of letting material obsessions influence your emotional needs.

Let's continue your reading. . .

How would you describe your knuckles?

INSTRUCTIONS: Look at your first and second knuckles and do your best to characterize them.

HINT: Don't just look at them. . .feel them!

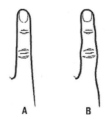

A. smooth (go to page 83)
B. knotty (go to page 84)

The bottom third

Close examination of your fingers reveals that you are very sensual. You enjoy eating and drinking, sometimes to excess. You are consumed with luxury and comfort.

Keep in mind that the thicker the base of your finger is, the more sensual you are. While this is often appreciated by your mate at the beginning of a relationship, if not kept in check it may be the source of future conflict.

Things are getting steamy, so let's continue your reading. . .

How flexible is the tip of your thumb?

INSTRUCTIONS: Hold your thumb in the air and bend the tip of your thumb back without any assistance from your other hand.

HINT: You are only determining the flexibility of the tip of your thumb.

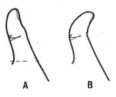

A. stiff (go to page 81)
B. flexible (go to page 82)

Stiff fingers
Your hand's flexibility is limited, therefore you are cautious, close-minded, and you lack adaptability. In relationships you may be conservative and avoid taking risks, such as making the first move.

You often find yourself intimidated by new ventures and new ideas and do not wish to venture out of the traditional boundaries established for love and romantic life, choosing a mate who shares your conservative tastes.

Let's continue your reading. . .

Where does your heart line begin?

INSTRUCTIONS: In general your heart line starts on the same side of your hand as your thumb. Select the answer that best describes the starting point of your heart line.

HINT: Hold your hand close to the light.

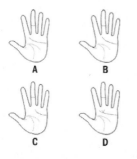

A. below the index finger (go to page 69)
B. between the index finger and middle finger (go to page 70)
C. below the middle finger (go to page 71)
D. branches from both fingers (go to page 72)

Now bend a little

You are balanced, even in action, and you have complete control of your-self. As a partner you listen well and understand the concerns of your mate.

Your natural tendency toward balance often finds you in relationships that are highly stable as you strive to avoid the extremes. As a partner you are neither held back by traditional ideas of relationships, nor rashly impelled to become a part of the latest romantic trend.

Let's continue your reading. . .

How flexible is the tip of your thumb?

INSTRUCTIONS: Hold your thumb in the air and bend the tip of your thumb back without any assistance from your other hand.

HINT: You are only determining the flexibility of the tip of your thumb.

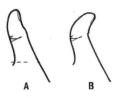

A. stiff (go to page 73)
B. flexible (go to page 74)

Let's get flexible

Your hands are extremely flexible and therefore so are your heart and mind. Ultimately, you are open to new ideas and willing to consider alternative perspectives in the realm of love and relationships.

Your romantic relationships may benefit from your ability to compromise and your overall spontaneity.

Let's continue your reading. . .

Where does your heart line begin?

INSTRUCTIONS: In general your heart line starts on the same side of your hand as your thumb. Select the answer that best describes the starting point of your heart line.

HINT: Hold your hand close to the light.

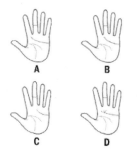

A. below the index finger (go to page 69)
B. between the index finger and middle finger (go to page 70)
C. below the middle finger (go to page 71)
D. branches from both fingers (go to page 72)

Long on top

Upon close examination of your fingers it is also clear that you are refined and have excellent taste in clothes, jewels, and luxurious home surroundings.

Your great taste will help you significantly if you are in search of romance. Everyone who meets you will be impressed by the way you present yourself.

Let's continue your reading. . .

How flexible is the tip of your thumb?

INSTRUCTIONS: Hold your thumb in the air and bend the tip of your thumb back without any assistance from your other hand.

HINT: You are only determining the flexibility of the tip of your thumb.

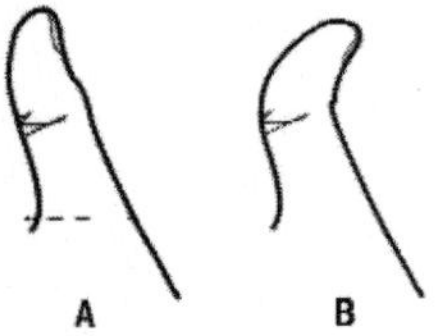

A. stiff (go to page 73)
B. flexible (go to page 74)

A   B

Long in the middle

Upon close examination of your fingers it is clear that you are most interested in making money. You are consumed with financial success.

You may discover that your satisfaction in a relationship is often determined by your financial standing. You may be in danger of letting material obsessions influence your emotional needs.

Let's continue your reading. . .

How would you describe your knuckles?

INSTRUCTIONS: Look at your first and second knuckles and do your best to characterize them.

HINT: Don't just look at them. . .feel them!

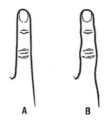

A. smooth (go to page 75)
B. knotty (go to page 76)

A   B

Long on the bottom
Upon close examination of your fingers it is clear that you are a healthy person with a genuine love of humankind. This probably explains why you are so well liked and have many friends.

However, you are changeable and not constant and this may cause tension in your relationships. You easily make enemies, as others are often jealous of you, and these often become bitter rivals. You are a great money-maker but you are not economical and are not concerned with saving your earnings.

Let's continue your reading. . .

How flexible is the tip of your thumb?

INSTRUCTIONS: Hold your thumb in the air and bend the tip of your thumb back without any assistance from your other hand.

HINT: You are only determining the flexibility of the tip of your thumb.

A. stiff (go to page 73)
B. flexible (go to page 74)

Stiff fingers

Your hand's flexibility is limited, therefore you are cautious, close-minded, and you lack adaptability. In relationships you may be conservative and avoid taking risks, such as making the first move.

You often find yourself intimidated by new ventures and new ideas and do not wish to venture out of the traditional boundaries established for love and romantic life, choosing a mate who shares your conservative tastes.

Let's continue your reading. . .

How would you describe your knuckles?

INSTRUCTIONS: Look at your first and second knuckles and do your best to characterize them.

HINT: Don't just look at them. . .feel them!

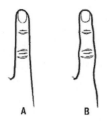

A. smooth (go to page 95)
B. knotty (go to page 96)

Now bend a little

You are balanced, even in action, and you have complete control of yourself. As a partner you listen well and understand the concerns of your mate.

Your natural tendency toward balance often finds you in relationships that are highly stable as you strive to avoid extremes. As a partner you are neither held back by traditional ideas of relationships, nor rashly impelled to become a part of the latest romantic trend.

Let's continue your reading. . .

Where does your heart line end?

INSTRUCTIONS: Your heart line should travel from someplace near your index finger toward the other side of your hand. Heart lines end in different places on everybody's hands.

HINT: Follow your heart line to the end.

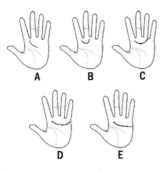

A. middle of the hand (go to page 97)
B. below the middle finger (go to page 98)
C. below the ring finger (go to page 99)
D. below the pinky finger (go to page 100)
E. other side of the palm (go to page 101)

Let's get flexible

Your hands are extremely flexible and therefore so are your heart and mind. Ultimately, you are open to new ideas and willing to consider alternative perspectives in the realm of love and relationships.

Your romantic relationships may benefit from your ability to compromise and your overall spontaneity.

Let's continue your reading. . .

How would you describe your knuckles?

INSTRUCTIONS: Look at your first and second knuckles and do your best to characterize them.

HINT: Don't just look at them. . .feel them!

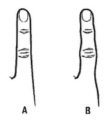

A. smooth (go to page 95)
B. knotty (go to page 96)

Long on top

Close examination of your fingers reveals that you are ruled by your head. You are absorbed in matters of the mind and you have a desire to be challenged intellectually. You tackle intellectual issues with exuberance and enjoy the company of fellow thinkers.

Let's continue your reading. . .

What color is your heart line?

INSTRUCTIONS: Open your hand and take a close look at your heart line running across the top of your hand. What shade do you think dominates your heart line?

HINT: Be sure to hold your hand under natural lighting.

A. pale (go to page 204)
B. pink (go to page 205)
C. red (go to page 206)
D. yellow (go to page 207)
E. blue (go to page 208)

Long in the middle

Close examination of your fingers reveals that you are most interested in making money. You are consumed with financial affairs.

You aggressively pursue material success and often achieve it through sheer determination. This may blind you to tending to your own emotional needs or the needs of those around you.

Let's continue your reading. . .

What color is your heart line?

INSTRUCTIONS: The heart line runs across the top of the palm. There is a wide range of heart line colors. It's up to you to determine which color best describes your heart line.

HINT: If you're with someone take a look at the difference between your heart lines.

A. pale (go to page 204)
B. pink (go to page 205)
C. red (go to page 206)
D. yellow (go to page 207)
E. blue (go to page 208)

Long on the bottom

Close examination of your fingers reveals that you are very sensual. You enjoy eating and drinking, sometimes to excess.

You are consumed with luxury and comfort and seek enjoyment with the exuberance that is typical of all your endeavors. While this may be appreciated by your partner at the outset, it may also be the source of problems if done in excess.

Let's continue your reading. . .

Does your heart line intersect with your head line or life line?

INSTRUCTIONS: Sometimes you will find a heart line that flows down toward the bottom of the hand. If it does it's likely that it will cross the head line and possibly even the life line. It may also merge with either of these lines.

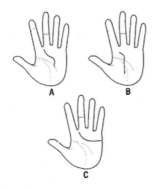

HINT: See if your heart line flows down your hand.

A. intersects with my head line (go to page 123)
B. intersects with my head line and life line (go to page 124)
C. none of the above (go to page 125)

You and your stiff fingers

Your hand's flexibility is limited, therefore you are cautious, close-minded, and you lack adaptability. In relationships you may be conservative and avoid taking risks, such as making the first move.

You often find yourself intimidated by new ventures and new ideas and do not wish to venture out of the traditional boundaries established for love and romantic life, choosing a mate who shares your conservative tastes.

Let's continue your reading. . .

How would you describe your knuckles?

INSTRUCTIONS: Look at your first and second knuckles and do your best to characterize them.

HINT: Don't just look at them. . .feel them!

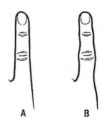

A. smooth (go to page 117)
B. knotty (go to page 118)

Let's bend a little
You are balanced, even in action, and you have complete control of yourself. As a partner you listen well and understand the concerns of your mate.

Your natural tendency toward balance often finds you in relationships that are highly stable as you strive to avoid extremes. As a partner you are neither held back by traditional ideas of relationships, nor rashly impelled to become a part of the latest romantic trend.

Let's continue your reading. . .

Where does your heart line begin?

INSTRUCTIONS: In general your heart line starts on the same side of your hand as your thumb. Select the answer that best describes the starting point of your heart line.

HINT: Hold your hand close to the light.

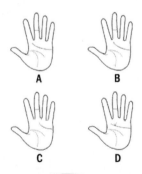

A. below the index finger (go to page 119)
B. between the index finger and middle finger (go to page 120)
C. below the middle finger (go to page 121)
D. branches from both fingers (go to page 122)

Let's get flexible

Your hands are extremely flexible and therefore so are your heart and mind. Ultimately, you are open to new ideas and willing to consider alternative perspectives in the realm of love and relationships.

Your romantic relationships may benefit from your ability to compromise and your overall spontaneity.

Let's continue your reading. . .

How would you describe your knuckles?

INSTRUCTIONS: Look at your first and second knuckles and do your best to characterize them.

HINT: Don't just look at them. . .feel them!

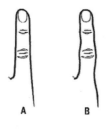

A. smooth (go to page 117)
B. knotty (go to page 118)

Long on top

Upon close examination of your fingers it is clear that you are refined and have excellent taste in clothes, jewels, and luxurious home surroundings.

Your strong first phalanx of your fingers also indicates a strong intuition, possibly even some psychic abilities. You should pay close attention to this intriguing quality.

Let's continue your reading. . .

Does your heart line intersect with your head line or life line?

INSTRUCTIONS: Sometimes you will find a heart line that flows down towards the bottom of the hand. If it does it's likely that it will cross the head line and possibly even the life line. It may also merge with either of these lines.

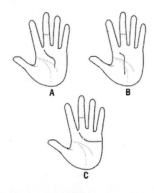

HINT: See if your heart line flows down your hand.

A. intersects with my head line (go to page 123)
B. intersects with my head line and life line (go to page 124)
C. none of the above (go to page 125)

Long in the middle

Upon close examination of your fingers it is clear that you are most interested in making money. You are consumed with financial success. You may discover that your satisfaction in a relationship is often determined by your financial standing.

You may be in danger of letting material obsessions influence your emotional needs.

Let's continue your reading. . .

What color is your heart line?

INSTRUCTIONS: The heart line runs across the top of the palm. There is a wide range of heart line colors. It's up to you to determine which color best describes your heart line.

HINT: If you're with someone take a look at the difference between your heart lines.

A. pale (go to page 199)
B. pink (go to page 200)
C. red (go to page 201)
D. yellow (go to page 202)
E. blue (go to page 203)

Long on the bottom

Upon close examination of your fingers it is clear that you are a healthy person with a genuine love of humankind, which probably explains why you are so well liked and have many friends. However, you are changeable and not constant and this may cause tension in your relationships. You easily make enemies, as others are often jealous of you, and these often become bitter rivals. You are a great money-maker but you are not economical and are not concerned with saving your earnings.

Let's continue your reading. . .

Does your heart line intersect with your head line or life line?

INSTRUCTIONS: Sometimes you will find a heart line that flows down towards the bottom of the hand. If it does it's likely that it will cross the head line and possibly even the life line. It may also merge with either of these lines.

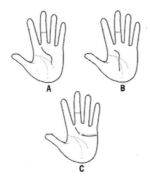

HINT: See if your heart line flows down your hand.

A. intersects with my head line (go to page 123)
B. intersects with my head line and life line (go to page 124)
C. none of the above (go to page 125)

Long on top

Close examination of your fingers reveals that you are a thinker who is inclined to believe in superstitions and the occult sciences. You are an intellectual with a student's curiosity. You enjoy the company of people who share your interest in mysticism.

What color is your heart line?

INSTRUCTIONS: The heart line runs across the top of the palm. There is a wide range of heart line colors. It's up to you to determine which color best describes your heart line.

HINT: If you're with someone take a look at the difference between your heart lines.

A. pale (go to page 85)
B. pink (go to page 86)
C. red (go to page 87)
D. yellow (go to page 88)
E. blue (go to page 89)

Long in the middle

Close examination of your fingers reveals that you have a strong business sense and will excel in the worlds of farming, agriculture, scientific investigations, chemistry, physics, history, and math. You will find monetary success in these fields and should be encouraged to do so.

What color is your heart line?

INSTRUCTIONS: The heart line runs across the top of the palm. There is a wide range of heart line colors. It's up to you to determine which color best describes your heart line.

HINT: If you're with someone take a look at the difference between your heart lines.

A. pale (go to page 85)
B. pink (go to page 86)
C. red (go to page 87)
D. yellow (go to page 88)
E. blue (go to page 89)

Long on the bottom
Close examination of your fingers reveals that you are economical. If this is not kept in check it can lead to money-worship and miserliness. If your third phalanx is thick, it means you are less studious, while if it is waist-like, it indicates that you will actively pursue research in your areas of interest.

What color is your heart line?

INSTRUCTIONS: The heart line runs across the top of the palm. There is a wide range of heart line colors. It's up to you to determine which color best describes your heart line.

HINT: If you're with someone take a look at the difference between your heart lines.

A. pale (go to page 85)
B. pink (go to page 86)
C. red (go to page 87)
D. yellow (go to page 88)
E. blue (go to page 89)

Long on top

Close examination of your fingers reveals that you are ruled by your head. You are an excellent decision maker and enjoy an atmosphere that stimulates and challenges your intellect. You enjoy the company of those with similar talents.

What color is your heart line?

INSTRUCTIONS: The heart line runs across the top of the palm. There is a wide range of heart line colors. It's up to you to determine which color best describes your heart line.

HINT: If you're with someone take a look at the difference between your heart lines.

A. pale (go to page 90)
B. pink (go to page 91)
C. red (go to page 92)
D. yellow (go to page 93)
E. blue (go to page 94)

Long in the middle

Close examination of your fingers reveals that you are most interested in making money. You are consumed with financial success and have the skills to attain it. If left unchecked this can lead to excessive materialism that could alienate you from others.

What color is your heart line?

INSTRUCTIONS: The heart line runs across the top of the palm. There is a wide range of heart line colors. It's up to you to determine which color best describes your heart line.

HINT: If you're with someone take a look at the difference between your heart lines.

A. pale (go to page 90)
B. pink (go to page 91)
C. red (go to page 92)
D. yellow (go to page 93)
E. blue (go to page 94)

Long on the bottom

Close examination of your fingers reveals that you are very sensual. You enjoy eating and drinking, sometimes to excess. You are consumed with luxury and comfort.

The thicker the bottom of your finger is, the more sensual you will be. While this is often appreciated by your mate at the beginning of a relationship, if not kept in check it may be the source of future conflict.

What color is your heart line?

INSTRUCTIONS: The heart line runs across the top of the palm. There is a wide range of heart line colors. It's up to you to determine which color best describes your heart line.

HINT: If you're with someone take a look at the difference between your heart lines.

A. pale (go to page 90)
B. pink (go to page 91)
C. red (go to page 92)
D. yellow (go to page 93)
E. blue (go to page 94)

Your heart's from Jupiter!

Since your heart line rises from the mount of Jupiter (below the index finger) you are extremely sentimental. Love is critical to your happiness.

You believe in the power of love. You would rather live in poverty with love, than with riches and an empty heart. You have a pure heart and a true understanding for compassion and commitment.

Does your heart line curve toward any fingers?

INSTRUCTIONS: As your heart line travels across your hand you may notice that it bends toward one of your fingers. Look to see which finger is directly above the bend. This would be your answer.

HINT: Look to see if your heart line has any significant curves.

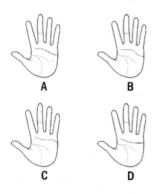

A. middle finger (go to page 152)
B. ring finger (go to page 153)
C. pinky finger (go to page 154)
D. none of the above (go to page 155)

Your heart's between your fingers!

Since your heart line rises between the mounts of Jupiter and Saturn (the index finger and middle finger) you fall in a "middle-ground" when it comes to affection.

You are not carried away with sentiment and you view love from a practical standpoint. You have a difficult time believing that a relationship can survive on love alone. You think that love in a cottage without plenty of bread and butter is a myth. You may be strong in affection, but you are not "foolish."

Where does your heart line end?

INSTRUCTIONS: Your heart line should travel from someplace near your index finger toward the other side of your hand. Heart lines end in different places on everybody's hands.

HINT: Follow your heart line to the end.

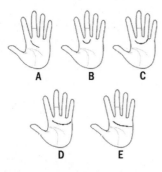

A. middle of the hand (go to page 156)
B. below the middle finger (go to page 157)
C. below the ring finger (go to page 158)
D. below the pinky finger (go to page 159)
E. other side of the palm (go to page 160)

Your heart rises from Saturn

Since your heart line rises from the mount of Saturn (below the middle finger) you are a sensualist. While you may not be as sensual as your Apollo friends, you still have your own strong sensual desires.

Love coupled with a strong attraction will set your heart and mind on fire. You live for personal satisfaction. You are consumed with your senses.

Does your heart line curve toward any fingers?

Instructions: As your heart line travels across your hand you may notice that it bends toward one of your fingers. Look to see which finger is directly above the bend. This would be your answer.

Hint: Look to see if your heart line has any significant curves.

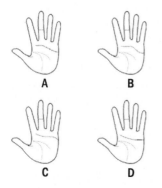

A. middle finger (go to page 152)
B. ring finger (go to page 153)
C. pinky finger (go to page 154)
D. none of the above (go to page 155)

Your heart's between your fingers!
Since your heart line rises from the mounts of both Jupiter and Saturn your heart represents the union of sentiment, common sense, and passion. You are a kind person with a warm heart.

You love your friends, all relationships, and humankind in general. Unfortunately, people have a habit of taking advantage of your charitable, loving attitude. You rarely look after your own interests when considering the interests of others. This selflessness is a great quality as long as you have great friends.

Where does your heart line end?

INSTRUCTIONS: Your heart line should travel from someplace near your index finger toward the other side of your hand. Heart lines end in different places on everybody's hands.

HINT: Follow your heart line to the end.

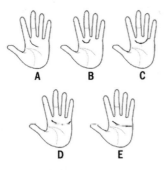

A. middle of the hand (go to page 156)
B. below the middle finger (go to page 157)
C. below the ring finger (go to page 158)
D. below the pinky finger (go to page 159)
E. other side of the palm (go to page 160)

An economical lover

Since your thumb is stiff you are practical, economical, stingy, and weigh everything carefully, all of which lessen the happy, congenial Apollonian influence.

You are both careful and determined and, at times, reluctant to trust others. You are even-tempered and have realistic expectations of others.

Does your heart line curve toward any fingers?

INSTRUCTIONS: As your heart line travels across your hand you may notice that it bends toward one of your fingers. Look to see which finger is directly above the bend. This would be your answer.

HINT: Look to see if your heart line has any significant curves.

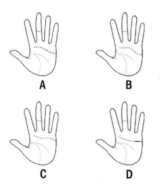

A

B

C

D

A. middle finger (go to page 152)
B. ring finger (go to page 153)
C. pinky finger (go to page 154)
D. none of the above (go to page 155)

A flexible lover

Since your thumb is supple and flexible you are brilliant and versatile, easily adapting yourself to changing circumstances. You achieve your successes in brilliant dashes and never seem to plod along.

Never satisfied to be led, you aspire to surpass your friends, and do so with ease, as you are extraordinarily talented. You have a most congenial and happy nature, as is expected of an Apollonian.

Where does your heart line end?

INSTRUCTIONS: Your heart line should travel from someplace near your index finger toward the other side of your hand. Heart lines end in different places on everybody's hands.

HINT: Follow your heart line to the end.

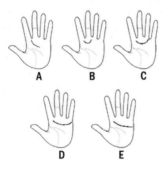

A. middle of the hand (go to page 156)
B. below the middle finger (go to page 157)
C. below the ring finger (go to page 158)
D. below the pinky finger (go to page 159)
E. other side of the palm (go to page 160)

Simply a smooth operator
Your smooth fingers are typical of the Apollonian. They indicate a love of the arts, impulsive behavior, and excellent intuition. These are the main sources of the Apollonian's strength.

Does your heart line curve toward any fingers?

INSTRUCTIONS: As your heart line travels across your hand you may notice that it bends toward one of your fingers. Look to see which finger is directly above the bend. This would be your answer.

HINT: Look to see if your heart line has any significant curves.

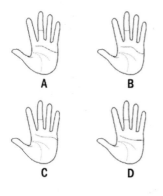

A. middle finger (go to page 152)
B. ring finger (go to page 153)
C. pinky finger (go to page 154)
D. none of the above (go to page 155)

Tied in knots

Your knotty finger joints are not common to the Apollonian. They serve to keep your enthusiasm and spontaneity in check.

You do not tend to be analytical, and your mental processes are quick and based more on intuition than reason. Since knotty fingers are not typical of your type, they may serve as a source of conflict with the other elements of your character.

Where does your heart line end?

INSTRUCTIONS: Your heart line should travel from someplace near your index finger toward the other side of your hand. Heart lines end in different places on everybody's hands.

HINT: Follow your heart line to the end.

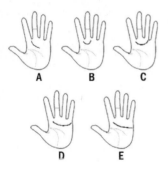

A. middle of the hand (go to page 156)
B. below the middle finger (go to page 157)
C. below the ring finger (go to page 158)
D. below the pinky finger (go to page 159)
E. other side of the palm (go to page 160)

Your heart's from Jupiter!

Since your heart line rises from the mount of Jupiter (below the index finger) you are extremely sentimental.

Love is critical to your happiness. You believe in the power of love. You would rather live in poverty with love, than with riches and an empty heart. You have a pure heart and a true understanding for compassion and commitment.

Which of the following terms best describes your skin texture?

INSTRUCTIONS: If you examine your hand closely you should be able to determine the texture of your skin. Soft skin will feel like a feather, elastic skin will have some spring, and coarse skin will feel rough. How's your skin feel?

HINT: Don't just look at your skin. . .touch it.

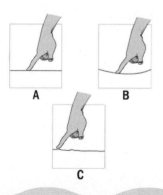

A. soft and fine (go to page 138)
B. elastic (go to page 139)
C. coarse (go to page 140)

Your heart's between your fingers!

Since your heart line rises between the mounts of Jupiter and Saturn (the index finger and middle finger) you fall in a "middle-ground" when it comes to affection.

You are not carried away with sentiment and you view love from a practical standpoint. You have a difficult time believing that a relationship can survive on love alone. You think that love in a cottage without plenty of bread and butter is a myth. You may be strong in affection, but you are not "foolish."

Which of the following terms best describes your skin texture?

INSTRUCTIONS: If you examine your hand closely you should be able to determine the texture of your skin. Soft skin will feel like a feather, elastic skin will have some spring, and coarse skin will feel rough. How's your skin feel?

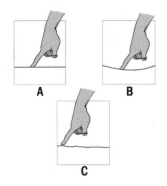

HINT: Don't just look at your skin. . .touch it.

A. soft and fine (go to page 138)
B. elastic (go to page 139)
C. coarse (go to page 140)

Your heart rises from Saturn
Since your heart line rises from the mount of Saturn (below the middle finger) you are a sensualist. You clearly have strong sensual desires.

Love coupled with a strong attraction will set your heart and mind on fire. You live for personal satisfaction. You are consumed with your senses.

Which of the following terms best describes your skin texture?
INSTRUCTIONS: If you examine your hand closely you should be able to determine the texture of your skin. Soft skin will feel like a feather, elastic skin will have some spring, and coarse skin will feel rough. How's your skin feel?

HINT: Don't just look at your skin. . .touch it.

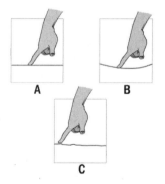

A. soft and fine (go to page 138)
B. elastic (go to page 139)
C. coarse (go to page 140)

Your heart's between your fingers!

Since your heart line rises from the mounts of both Jupiter and Saturn your heart represents the union of sentiment, common sense, and passion. You are a kind person with a warm heart.

You love your friends, all relationships, and humankind in general. Unfortunately, people have a habit of taking advantage of your charitable, loving attitude. You rarely look after your own interests when considering the interests of others. This selflessness is a great quality as long as you have great friends.

Which of the following terms best describes your skin texture?

INSTRUCTIONS: If you examine your hand closely you should be able to determine the texture of your skin. Soft skin will feel like a feather, elastic skin will have some spring, and coarse skin will feel rough. How's your skin feel?

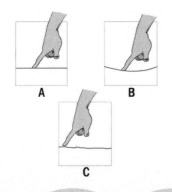

HINT: Don't just look at your skin. . .touch it.

A. soft and fine (go to page 138)
B. elastic (go to page 139)
C. coarse (go to page 140)

An economical lover

Since your thumb is stiff you are practical, wise, and weigh everything carefully. You are strong-willed, determined, and exercise great caution and reserve.

Unlike most Jupiterians, you have difficulty trusting others, and you may also appear to be untrustworthy yourself. A stiff thumb also indicates you are steady and even-tempered and do not expect much from others, making you less susceptible to disappointment.

Do you have any lines on the side of your hand below your pinky?

INSTRUCTIONS: If you make a loose fist and look at the side of your hand between your pinky finger and your heart line you may notice some lines. These lines of affection are usually easily found, but on some rare occasions you may not find any.

HINT: Make a fist and examine the side of your hand.

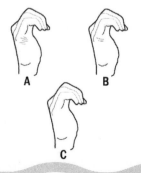

A. three or more (go to page 141)
B. one or two (go to page 142)
C. none (go to page 143)

Rubber thumb

Since your thumb is supple and flexible you demonstrate brilliance, versatility, and easily adapt yourself to changing circumstances. You are extremely generous and also emotional.

You are deeply affected by matters of the heart, but with the balanced influence of the Jupiterian, you manage to maintain your happy disposition in most circumstances.

Which of the following terms best describes your skin texture?

INSTRUCTIONS: If you examine your hand closely you should be able to determine the texture of your skin. Soft skin will feel like a feather, elastic skin will have some spring, and coarse skin will feel rough. How's your skin feel?

HINT: Don't just look at your skin. . .touch it.

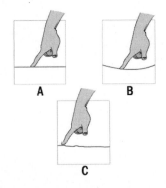

A. soft and fine (go to page 138)
B. elastic (go to page 139)
C. coarse (go to page 140)

A

B

C

Smooth operator

Additionally, you possess some significant artistic traits. You act on impulse, inspiration, and intuition. You tend to make decisions with your heart instead of your head.

You express yourself well and you are comfortable in almost all social surroundings.

Do you have any lines on the side of your hand below your pinky?

INSTRUCTIONS: If you make a loose fist and look at the side of your hand between your pinky finger and your heart line you may notice some lines. These lines of affection are usually easily found, but on some rare occasions you may not find any.

HINT: Make a fist and examine the side of your hand.

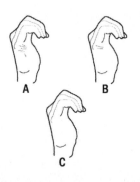

A. three or more (go to page 141)
B. one or two (go to page 142)
C. none (go to page 143)

Tied in knots

Your knotty finger joints indicate that you are philosophical. Since you also have square fingertips you are a disciplinarian and a "taskmaster."

This combination may create friction in your relationships. Your insistence on getting to the bottom of everything may be a point of tension for you and your mate. You are led by your head and not your heart.

Which of the following terms best describes your skin texture?

INSTRUCTIONS: If you examine your hand closely you should be able to determine the texture of your skin. Soft skin will feel like a feather, elastic skin will have some spring, and coarse skin will feel rough. How's your skin feel?

HINT: Don't just look at your skin. . .touch it.

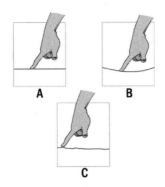

A. soft and fine (go to page 138)
B. elastic (go to page 139)
C. coarse (go to page 140)

A pale heart line

You may have a heart line, but its pale coloring may leave you feeling cold and lonely. You are certain to have trouble finding love, and even when you've found it you may struggle to keep it.

Don't surrender to the symbols and signs found on your hand. You control your own destiny. If you are serious about improving your love life just make the extra effort. Over time you'll notice that your pale lines will turn to pink!

Let's continue your reading. . .

How would you describe the texture of your heart line?

INSTRUCTIONS: Examine your heart line very closely. A smooth, clear line is not very common. More often than not your lines will consist of an interesting pattern. Do you see a pattern?

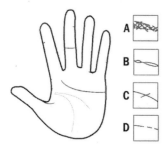

HINT: Take a good look at your lines.

A. chained (go to page 144)
B. islands (go to page 145)
C. crossed (go to page 146)
D. broken (go to page 147)

Pretty in pink

Your pink heart line is a pleasant reward for being compassionate and warm. As long as your heart line retains this shading you are sure to be a true romantic.

You are unlikely to fall in love with someone who holds a pale heart line, but if you do it's certain that your affection will turn his or her heart line pink.

Let's continue your reading. . .

Where does your heart line begin?

INSTRUCTIONS: In general your heart line starts on the same side of your hand as your thumb. Select the answer that best describes the starting point of your heart line.

HINT: Hold your hand close to the light.

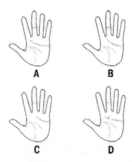

A. below the index finger (go to page 148)
B. between the index finger and middle finger (go to page 149)
C. below the middle finger (go to page 150)
D. branches from both fingers (go to page 151)

Red hot!

Your red heart line is a sign of unbridled passion and extreme desires. You are overwhelmed with emotion and you have a difficult time keeping your feelings to yourself. You may want to slow down.

Too much of anything can be dangerous, and in this case you may end up scaring away some terrific opportunities for romance.

Let's continue your reading. . .

How would you describe the texture of your heart line?

INSTRUCTIONS: Examine your heart line very closely. A smooth, clear line is not very common. More often than not your lines will consist of an interesting pattern. Do you see a pattern?

HINT: Take a good look at your lines.

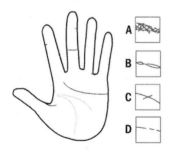

A. chained (go to page 144)
B. islands (go to page 145)
C. crossed (go to page 146)
D. broken (go to page 147)

A yellow heart?

Your yellow heart line may be a sign of trouble. You may just be turned off by romance and everything it entails. You appear to be content with solitude and your individual needs.

At this moment the idea of providing for anyone else is very unappealing for you. You aren't selfish, you're just not sure if you're ready for romance. The single life may be best for you right now.

Let's continue your reading. . .

How would you describe the texture of your heart line?

INSTRUCTIONS: Examine your heart line very closely. A smooth, clear line is not very common. More often than not your lines will consist of an interesting pattern. Do you see a pattern?

HINT: Take a good look at your lines.

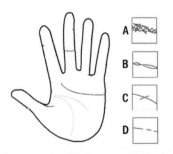

A. chained (go to page 144)
B. islands (go to page 145)
C. crossed (go to page 146)
D. broken (go to page 147)

A heart with the blues

Your blue heart line indicates that you may be struggling with your love life. You're having a difficult time making decisions. You are confused.

It's healthy to think things through, but you may be thinking a bit too much. The stress may begin to overwhelm you and your personal health may suffer. Relax and go with your feelings. Don't be afraid to make a mistake.

Let's continue your reading. . .

How would you describe the texture of your heart line?

INSTRUCTIONS: Examine your heart line very closely. A smooth, clear line is not very common. More often than not your lines will consist of an interesting pattern. Do you see a pattern?

HINT: Take a good look at your lines.

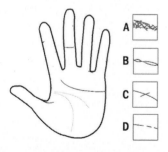

A. chained (go to page 144)
B. islands (go to page 145)
C. crossed (go to page 146)
D. broken (go to page 147)

A pale heart line

You may have a heart line, but its pale coloring may leave you feeling cold and lonely. You are certain to have trouble finding love, and even when you've found it you may struggle to keep it.

Don't surrender to the symbols and signs found on your hand. You control your own destiny. If you are serious about improving your love life just make the extra effort. Over time you'll notice that your pale lines will turn to pink!

Let's continue your reading. . .

How would you describe the base of your fingers?

INSTRUCTIONS: If you relax your hand and hold it directly in the light you will be able to determine the shape of the base of your fingers. They will either pinch in and be "waist-like" or they will flow straight down and be "long and thick." Good luck!

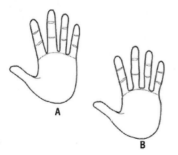

HINT: Relax your hand and hold it in the light.

A. long and thick (go to page 161)
B. narrow and waist-like (go to page 162)

Pretty in pink

Your pink heart line is a pleasant reward for being compassionate and warm. As long as your heart line retains this shading you are sure to be a true romantic.

You are unlikely to fall in love with someone who holds a pale heart line, but if you do it's certain that your affection will turn his or her heart line pink.

Let's continue your reading. . .

How would you describe the texture of your heart line?

INSTRUCTIONS: Examine your heart line very closely. A smooth, clear line is not very common. More often than not your lines will consist of an interesting pattern. Do you see a pattern?

HINT: Take a good look at your lines.

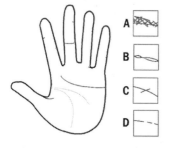

A. chained (go to page 163)
B. islands (go to page 164)
C. crossed (go to page 165)
D. broken (go to page 166)

Red hot!

Your red heart line is a sign of unbridled passion and extreme desires. You are overwhelmed with emotion and you have a difficult time keeping your feelings to yourself.

You may want to slow down. Too much of anything can be dangerous, and in this case you may end up scaring away some terrific opportunities for romance.

Let's continue your reading. . .

How would you describe the base of your fingers?

INSTRUCTIONS: If you relax your hand and hold it directly in the light you will be able to determine the shape of the base of your fingers. They will either pinch in and be "waist-like" or they will flow straight down and be "long and thick." Good luck!

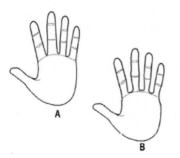

HINT: Relax your hand and hold it in the light.

A. long and thick (go to page 161)
B. narrow and waist-like (go to page 162)

A yellow heart?

Your yellow heart line may be a sign of trouble. You may just be turned off by romance and everything it entails. You appear to be content with solitude and your individual needs.

At this moment the idea of providing for anyone else is very unappealing for you. You aren't selfish, you're just not sure if you're ready for romance. The single life may be best for you right now.

Let's continue your reading. . .

How would you describe the texture of your heart line?

INSTRUCTIONS: Examine your heart line very closely. A smooth, clear line is not very common. More often than not your lines will consist of an interesting pattern. Do you see a pattern?

HINT: Take a good look at your lines.

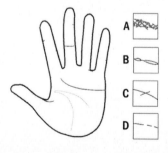

A. chained (go to page 163)
B. islands (go to page 164)
C. crossed (go to page 165)
D. broken (go to page 166)

A heart with the blues

Your blue heart line indicates that you may be struggling with your love life. You're having a difficult time making decisions. You are confused.

It's healthy to think things through, but you may be thinking a bit too much. The stress may begin to overwhelm you and your personal health may suffer. Relax and go with your feelings. Don't be afraid to make a mistake.

Let's continue your reading. . .

How would you describe the base of your fingers?

INSTRUCTIONS: If you relax your hand and hold it directly in the light you will be able to determine the shape of the base of your fingers. They will either pinch in and be "waist-like" or they will flow straight down and be "long and thick." Good luck!

HINT: Relax your hand and hold it in the light.

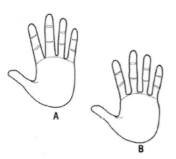

A. long and thick (go to page 161)
B. narrow and waist-like (go to page 162)

Smooth operator

Additionally, you possess some significant artistic traits. You act on impulse, inspiration, and intuition. You tend to make decisions with your heart instead of your head.

You express yourself well and you are comfortable in almost all social surroundings.

Let's continue your reading. . .

Which two fingers have the most space between them?

INSTRUCTIONS: Relax your hand and hold it in front of you. Hold your fingers out in their most natural and comfortable position. Now you can see if your fingers are spaced evenly.

HINT: Be sure to relax your hand.

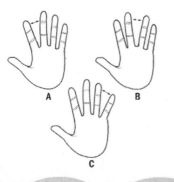

A. index finger and middle finger
  (go to page 130)
B. middle finger and ring finger
  (go to page 131)
C. ring finger and pinky finger
  (go to page 132)

Tied in knots

Your knotty finger joints indicate that you are philosophical. Since you also have square fingertips you are a disciplinarian and a "taskmaster."

This combination may create friction in your relationships. Your insistence on coldly getting to the bottom of everything may be a point of tension for you and your mate. You are led by your head and not your heart.

Let's continue your reading. . .

Which two fingers have the most space between them?

INSTRUCTIONS: Relax your hand and hold it in front of you. Hold your fingers out in their most natural and comfortable position. Now you can see if your fingers are spaced evenly.

HINT: Be sure to relax your hand.

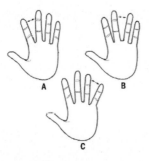

A. index finger and middle finger
   (go to page 130)
B. middle finger and ring finger
   (go to page 131)
C. ring finger and pinky finger
   (go to page 132)

Your heart in the middle of your hand

We continue our reading of the heart line by examining the length of the line as well as the location on your hand where the heart line terminates. Your heart line ends close to the middle of your hand. This is interesting, since your heart line is not strongly influenced by any of the major mounts. The length of your heart line indicates that while you are loving, you are also practical. You make wise, confident decisions related to love. You are ready for just about anything and you welcome the emotions that come with a strong relationship.

Let's continue your reading. . .

Which third of your hand is the most pronounced?

INSTRUCTIONS: Your hand is divided into three sections: the upper, middle, and lower. Use the image to assist you in determining which section of your hand is most pronounced. This isn't always easy to do. Answer to the best of your ability.

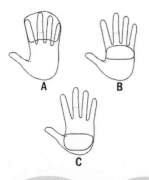

HINT: Decide which section of your hand dominates.

A. upper third (go to page 110)
B. middle third (go to page 111)
C. lower third (go to page 112)

Your heart goes to Saturn!

We continue our reading of the heart line by examining where the heart line appears to terminate. Your heart line terminates close to the mount of Saturn below your middle finger. This means several things. Since your heart line is quite short you are usually a bit cold and "heartless." You were born with a good heart, but time has had an impact on your affection. In addition, since your heart line ends below your middle finger, Saturnian qualities are beginning to take control of your heart. Most noticeable are the Saturnian's lack of emotion and indifference.

Let's continue your reading. . .

Which third of your hand is the most pronounced?

INSTRUCTIONS: Your hand is divided into three sections: the upper, middle, and lower. Use the image to assist you in determining which section of your hand is most pronounced. This isn't always easy to do. Answer to the best of your ability.

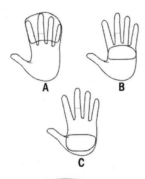

HINT: Decide which section of your hand dominates.

A. upper third (go to page 110)
B. middle third (go to page 111)
C. lower third (go to page 112)

Ring (finger) around your heart

We continue our reading of the heart line by examining the length of the line as well as the location on your hand where the heart line appears to terminate. Your heart line terminates close to the mount of Apollo, just below your ring finger.

You are attracted to the Apollonian ideas of beauty and art. You are consumed with beauty and in marriage you are likely to be unhappy unless you find someone with your same ideals. Your ideal mate will have a heart line that behaves much like yours.

Which third of your hand is the most pronounced?

INSTRUCTIONS: Your hand is divided into three sections: the upper, middle, and lower. Use the image to assist you in determining which section of your hand is most pronounced. This isn't always easy to do. Answer to the best of your ability.

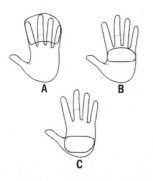

HINT: Decide which section of your hand dominates.

A. upper third (go to page 110)
B. middle third (go to page 111)
C. lower third (go to page 112)

Your heart goes to Mercury!

We continue our reading of the heart line by examining the length of the line as well as the location on your hand where the heart line appears to terminate. Your heart line terminates close to the mount of Mercury, just below your pinky finger. This means that finances largely influence your affections.

The Mercurian shrewdness guides this heart line; therefore money must always be in sight before love is recognized. When you love your love is strong, but you don't act on impulsive affection.

Which third of your hand is the most pronounced?

INSTRUCTIONS: Your hand is divided into three sections: the upper, middle, and lower. Use the image to assist you in determining which section of your hand is most pronounced. This isn't always easy to do. Answer to the best of your ability.

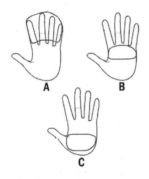

HINT: Decide which section of your hand dominates.

A. upper third (go to page 110)
B. middle third (go to page 111)
C. lower third (go to page 112)

A long heart line

We continue our reading of the heart line by examining the length of the line as well as the location on your hand where the heart line appears to terminate. Your heart line terminates all the way on the other side of your palm. You bring a new meaning to the word affection.

You have too much heart and you allow sentiment to guide you in everything. You easily become jealous and you will suffer if the love you share with others is not returned. Some palmists have read this line as a sign that you will "fail in all enterprises." This is not accurate. You simply need to be more careful about sharing your compassion only with those who really deserve it.

Which third of your hand is the most pronounced?

INSTRUCTIONS: Your hand is divided into three sections: the upper, middle, and lower. Use the image to assist you in determining which section of your hand is most pronounced. This isn't always easy to do. Answer to the best of your ability.

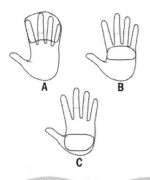

HINT: Decide which section of your hand dominates.

A. upper third (go to page 110)
B. middle third (go to page 111)
C. lower third (go to page 112)

Long on top

Close examination of your fingers reveals that you are ruled by your mind. You are absorbed with mental matters and you deserve a partner with the same intellectual expectations. There is nothing more disappointing to you than a date with a "box of rocks."

Maybe you should seek out a local library. In fact consider joining a book club. If you can't find one there's no reason you can't start one of your own. It could be your proactive approach to dating!

Let's continue your reading. . .

What color is your heart line?

INSTRUCTIONS: Closely examine your heart line under the light and do your best to determine its shading.

HINT: Hold your hand under the light.

A. pale (go to page 105)
B. pink (go to page 106)
C. red (go to page 107)
D. yellow (go to page 108)
E. blue (go to page 109)

Long in the middle

Close examination of your fingers reveals that you are most interested in making money. This may interfere with your pursuit of love. Although you enjoy making money you aren't so keen on spending it.

In some cases you will find people drawn to your money only to realize that you aren't going to shower them with expensive gifts. Do your best to avoid lovers who fail to look beyond your bank account.

Let's continue your reading. . .

What color is your heart line?

INSTRUCTIONS: Closely examine your heart line under the light and do your best to determine its shading.

HINT: Hold your hand under the light.

A. pale (go to page 105)
B. pink (go to page 106)
C. red (go to page 107)
D. yellow (go to page 108)
E. blue (go to page 109)

Long on the bottom

Close examination of your fingers reveals that you are very sensual. You enjoy eating and drinking, occasionally to excess.

You are attracted to people and places that appeal to the senses and may find that you get carried away in your pursuit of pleasure. While this may make you many new friends initially, it may serve to alienate you from those you love.

Let's continue your reading. . .

What color is your heart line?

INSTRUCTIONS: Closely examine your heart line under the light and do your best to determine its shading.

HINT: Hold your hand under the light.

A. pale (go to page 105)
B. pink (go to page 106)
C. red (go to page 107)
D. yellow (go to page 108)
E. blue (go to page 109)

A *pale heart line*

You may have a heart line, but its pale coloring may leave you feeling cold and lonely. You are certain to have trouble finding love, and even when you've found it you may struggle to keep it.

Don't surrender to the symbols and signs found on your hand. You control your own destiny. If you are serious about improving your love life just make the extra effort. Over time you'll notice that your pale lines will turn to pink!

Let's continue your reading. . .

How would you describe the texture of your heart line?

INSTRUCTIONS: Examine your heart line very closely. A smooth, clear line is not very common. More often than not your lines will consist of an interesting pattern. Do you see a pattern?

HINT: Take a good look at your lines.

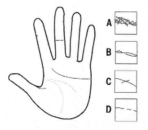

A. chained (go to page 209)
B. islands (go to page 210)
C. crossed (go to page 211)
D. broken (go to page 212)

Pretty in pink

Your pink heart line is a pleasant reward for being compassionate and warm. As long as your heart line retains this shading you are sure to be a true romantic.

You are unlikely to fall in love with someone who holds a pale heart line, but if you do it's certain that your affection will turn his or her heart line pink.

Let's continue your reading. . .

Where does your heart line begin?

INSTRUCTIONS: In general your heart line starts on the same side of your hand as your thumb. In this question we are trying to determine precisely where it starts. Select the answer that best describes the starting point of your heart line.

HINT: Hold your hand close to the light.

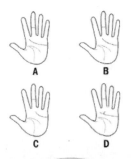

A. below the index finger (go to page 126)
B. between the index finger and middle finger (go to page 127)
C. below the middle finger (go to page 128)
D. branches from both fingers (go to page 129)

Red hot!
Your red heart line is a sign of unbridled passion and extreme desires. You are overwhelmed with emotion and you have a difficult time keeping your feelings to yourself.

You may want to slow down. Too much of anything can be dangerous, and in this case you may end up scaring away some terrific opportunities for romance.

Let's continue your reading. . .

How would you describe the texture of your heart line?

INSTRUCTIONS: Examine your heart line very closely. A smooth, clear line is not very common. More often than not your lines will consist of an interesting pattern. Do you see a pattern?

HINT: Take a good look at your lines.

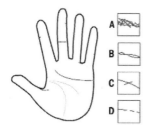

A. chained(go to page 209)
B. islands (go to page 210)
C. crossed (go to page 211)
D. broken (go to page 212)

A yellow heart?

Your yellow heart line may be a sign of trouble. You may just be turned off by romance and everything it entails. You appear to be content with solitude and your individual needs.

At this moment the idea of providing for anyone else is very unappealing for you. You aren't selfish, you're just not sure if you're ready for romance. The single life may be best for you right now.

Let's continue your reading. . .

Where does your heart line begin?

INSTRUCTIONS: In general your heart line starts on the same side of your hand as your thumb. In this question we are trying to determine precisely where it starts. Select the answer that best describes the starting point of your heart line.

HINT: Hold your hand close to the light.

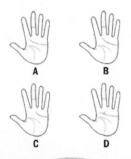

A. below the index finger (go to page 126)
B. between the index finger and middle finger (go to page 127)
C. below the middle finger (go to page 128)
D. branches from both fingers (go to page 129)

A heart with the blues

Your blue heart line indicates that you may be struggling with your love life. You're having a difficult time making decisions. You are confused. It's healthy to think things through, but you may be thinking a bit too much.

The stress may begin to overwhelm you and your personal health may suffer. Relax and go with your feelings. Don't be afraid to make a mistake.

Let's continue your reading. . .

How would you describe the texture of your heart line?

INSTRUCTIONS: Examine your heart line very closely. A smooth, clear line is not very common. More often than not your lines will consist of an interesting pattern. Do you see a pattern?

HINT: Take a good look at your lines.

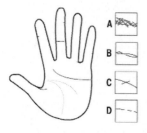

A. chained (go to page 209)
B. islands (go to page 210)
C. crossed (go to page 211)
D. broken (go to page 212)

The upper third

The upper third of your hand is dominant which is a sign that you are consumed with love. As is typical of the Martian type, your sympathy is lofty and your generosity is boundless.

You enjoy music, poetry, and romance, and your superior intellect influences your outlook on all aspects of life. You should be careful, however, since your generosity may sometimes be undeserved. Your giving spirit may be taken advantage of if not genuinely appreciated by your mate.

Let's continue your reading. . .

How would you describe the shading of your palm?

Instructions: Your palm could have just about any shading to it. Hold your hand flat and look to see if you have a tinge of color in your palm. Look at your entire palm and determine what the general shading is.

HINT: Use the shades below as a reference.

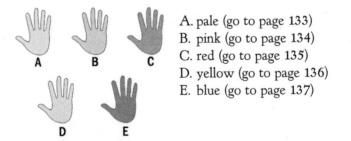

A. pale (go to page 133)
B. pink (go to page 134)
C. red (go to page 135)
D. yellow (go to page 136)
E. blue (go to page 137)

The middle third

The middle portion of your hand is most prominent, which is a sign that you are often consumed with business and practical affairs, since here rest the centers of ambition, sobriety, and aggression. As a Martian, you are full of fight, push, and energy, and never seem to be discouraged. Thus, you may find yourself best suited for a commercial position, politics, agricultural pursuits, or anything that is entirely practical. You are motivated by money, and you live in the world of material matters. You appreciate a mate that shares these values and attitudes.

Let's continue your reading. . .

How would you describe the shading of your palm?

Instructions: Your palm could have just about any shading to it. Hold your hand flat and look to see if you have a tinge of color in your palm. Look at your entire palm and determine what the general shading is.

HINT: Use the shades below as a reference.

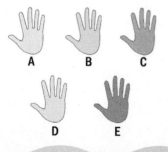

A. pale (go to page 133)
B. pink (go to page 134)
C. red (go to page 135)
D. yellow (go to page 136)
E. blue (go to page 137)

The lower third

The lower part of your hand is most prominent, which is a sign that you are more concerned with quantity than quality. You prefer a hearty meal to a gourmet meal that is less filling. In extreme cases, as a Martian type you may become vulgar and focus on base desires that can lead to crime.

Romantically, in striving to get the most instead of the best, you may end up shortchanging yourself and find that there is an element missing in your life. You may find that the happiness of the balanced life eludes you.

Let's continue your reading. . .

How would you describe the shading of your palm?

INSTRUCTIONS: Your palm could have just about any shading to it. Hold your hand flat and look to see if you have a tinge of color in your palm. Look at your entire palm and determine what the general shading is.

HINT: Use the shades below as a reference.

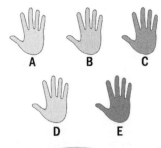

A. pale (go to page 133)
B. pink (go to page 134)
C. red (go to page 135)
D. yellow (go to page 136)
E. blue (go to page 137)

The sentimental heart

The effect of the chained lines on your hand is the weak operation of the qualities of the line. If chains are seen on only part of a line, the weak, poor operation of the line will occur. The chains make it impossible for your current to flow freely and evenly through the line, creating a labored, strained, obstructed condition. If the chain appears on your heart line you may be more sentimental than those around you. You may also have a tendency to become nervous and uncomfortable in risky relationships.

Let's continue your reading. . .

How would you describe the shading of your palm?

INSTRUCTIONS: Your palm could have just about any shading to it. Hold your hand flat and look to see if you have a tinge of color in your palm. Look at your entire palm and determine what the general shading is.

HINT: Use the shades below as a reference.

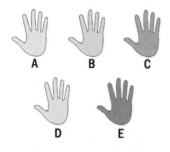

A. pale (go to page 133)
B. pink (go to page 134)
C. red (go to page 135)
D. yellow (go to page 136)
E. blue (go to page 137)

Labored love

The island formation on the lines of your hand divides the strength of the current, producing a consequent division of strength and force thus lessening their vital force. If you find significant islands on your heart line you will face some challenging times in your love life.

Let's continue your reading. . .

Where does your heart line end?

INSTRUCTIONS: Your heart line should travel from someplace near your index finger toward the other side of your hand. Heart lines end in different places on everybody's hands.

HINT: Follow your heart line to the end.

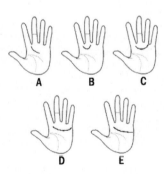

A. middle of the hand (go to page 97)
B. below the middle finger (go to page 98)
C. below the ring finger (go to page 99)
D. below the pinky finger (go to page 100)
E. other side of the palm (go to page 101)

A crossed heart

The crossed lines that appear on your hands are a common sign. A deep-cut cross is a sign of grave importance, especially if highly colored. The cross is an obstacle or a defect, and can produce a bad quality or a change in the course of your love life. Imagine the current of love running through your heart line. When your heart line crosses another line the strength of the line is diminished. Subsequently your heart line reflects a dwindling passion.

Let's continue your reading. . .

Where does your heart line end?

INSTRUCTIONS: Your heart line should travel from someplace near your index finger toward the other side of your hand. Heart lines end in different places on everybody's hands.

HINT: Follow your heart line to the end.

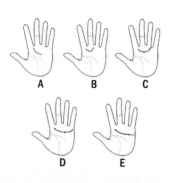

A. middle of the hand (go to page 97)
B. below the middle finger (go to page 98)
C. below the ring finger (go to page 99)
D. below the pinky finger (go to page 100)
E. other side of the palm (go to page 101)

A broken line

The breaks in the lines on your hand are frequently encountered and often indicate a defective condition. It signifies that the current is interrupted and stopped in exactly the same manner as when a telephone wire is cut. In some cases, the lines may eventually grow together or the current may jump over the break.

The wider the break, the more serious it becomes and the less likelihood there is of the current's passing over the space between the broken ends. The effects of this may be felt in your love life if the breaks are on the heart line and your head line.

Where does your heart line end?

INSTRUCTIONS: Your heart line should travel from someplace near your index finger toward the other side of your hand. Heart lines end in different places on everybody's hands.

HINT: Follow your heart line to the end.

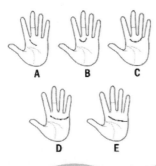

A. middle of the hand (go to page 97)
B. below the middle finger (go to page 98)
C. below the ring finger (go to page 99)
D. below the pinky finger (go to page 100)
E. other side of the palm (go to page 101)

Smooth Operator

Additionally, you possess some significant artistic traits. You act on impulse, inspiration, and intuition. You tend to make decisions with your heart instead of your head. You express yourself well and you are comfortable in almost all social surroundings.

Do you have any lines on the side of your hand below your pinky?

INSTRUCTIONS: If you make a loose fist and look at the side of your hand between your pinky finger and your heart line you may notice some lines. These lines of affection are usually easily found, but on some rare occasions they may be completely missing.

HINT: Make a fist and examine the side of your hand.

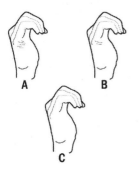

A. three or more (go to page 167)
B. one or two (go to page 168)
C. none (go to page 169)

Tied in knots

Your knotty finger joints indicate that you are philosophical. In your constant attempts to get to the bottom of everything you may become remote and moody. You are led by your head and not your heart. You often over-examine your relationships and tend to trouble yourself and your partner over issues that may not always be relevant.

Do you have any lines on the side of your hand below your pinky?

INSTRUCTIONS: If you make a loose fist and look at the side of your hand between your pinky finger and your heart line you may notice some lines. These lines of affection are usually easily found, but on some rare occasions they may be completely missing.

HINT: Make a fist and examine the side of your hand.

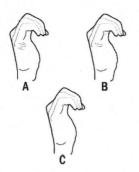

A. three or more (go to page 167)
B. one or two (go to page 168)
C. none (go to page 169)

Your heart's from Jupiter!

Now we can examine the starting point of your heart line. Since your heart line rises from the mount of Jupiter (below the index finger) you are extremely sentimental. Love is critical to your happiness.

You believe in the power of love. You would rather live in poverty with love, than with riches and an empty heart. You have a pure heart and a true understanding for compassion and commitment.

Let's continue your reading. . .

Where does your heart line end?

INSTRUCTIONS: Your heart line should travel from someplace near your index finger toward the other side of your hand. Heart lines end in different places on everybody's hands. Where does your heart line end?

HINT: Follow your heart line to the end.

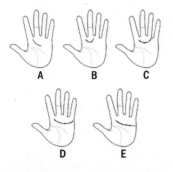

A. middle of the hand (go to page 170)
B. below the middle finger (go to page 171)
C. below the ring finger (go to page 172)
D. below the pinky finger (go to page 173)
E. other side of the palm (go to page 174)

Your heart's between your fingers

Now we can examine the starting point of your heart line. Since your heart line rises between the mounts of Jupiter and Saturn (the index finger and middle finger) you fall in a "middle-ground" when it comes to affection.

You view love from a practical standpoint. You have a difficult time believing that a relationship can survive on love alone. You think that love in a cottage without plenty of bread and butter is a myth. You may be strong in affection, but you are not "foolish."

Let's continue your reading. . .

Where does your heart line end?

INSTRUCTIONS: Your heart line should travel from someplace near your index finger toward the other side of your hand. Heart lines end in different places on everybody's hands.

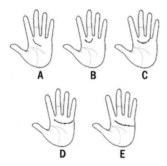

HINT: Follow your heart line to the end.

A. middle of the hand (go to page 170)
B. below the middle finger (go to page 171)
C. below the ring finger (go to page 172)
D. below the pinky finger (go to page 173)
E. other side of the palm (go to page 174)

Your heart rises from Saturn!

Now we can examine the starting point of your heart line. Since your heart line rises from the mount of Saturn (below the middle finger) you are a sensualist. While you may not be as sensual as your Apollo friends, you still have your own strong sensual desires.

Love coupled with a strong attraction will set your heart and mind on fire. You live for personal satisfaction. You are consumed with your senses.

Let's continue your reading. . .

Where does your heart line end?

INSTRUCTIONS: Your heart line should travel from someplace near your index finger toward the other side of your hand. Heart lines end in different places on everybody's hands.

HINT: Follow your heart line to the end.

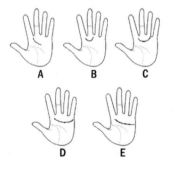

A. middle of the hand (go to page 170)
B. below the middle finger (go to page 171)
C. below the ring finger (go to page 172)
D. below the pinky finger (go to page 173)
E. other side of the palm (go to page 174)

Your heart's between your fingers

Now we can examine the starting point of your heart line. Since your heart line rises from the mounts of both Jupiter and Saturn your heart represents the union of sentiment, common sense, and passion. You are a kind person with a warm heart.

You love your friends, all relationships, and humankind in general. Unfortunately, people have a habit of taking advantage of your charitable, loving attitude. You rarely look after your own interests when considering the interests of others. This selflessness is a great quality as long as you have great friends.

Let's continue your reading. . .

Where does your heart line end?

INSTRUCTIONS: Your heart line should travel from someplace near your index finger toward the other side of your hand. Heart lines end in different places on everybody's hands.

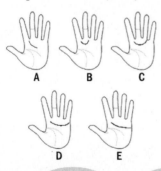

A   B   C

D   E

HINT: Follow your heart line to the end.

A. middle of the hand (go to page 170)
B. below the middle finger (go to page 171)
C. below the ring finger (go to page 172)
D. below the pinky finger (go to page 173)
E. other side of the palm (go to page 174)

Your heart runs into your head

You have indicated that your heart line intersects your head line. This is a troubling discovery, as it reflects your inability to maintain stability in your relationships. Subsequently, you might have a tendency to overanalyze your relationships and this may ultimately lead you to have trouble finding a long-lasting romance. You may want to take more time to step back and enjoy the little things. Try not to overanalyze the romantic behavior of your lover.

Do you have any lines on the side of your hand below your pinky?

INSTRUCTIONS: If you make a loose fist and look at the side of your hand between your pinky finger and your heart line you may notice some lines. These lines of affection are usually easily found, but on some rare occasions they may be completely missing.

HINT: Make a fist and examine the side of your hand.

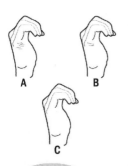

A. three or more (go to page 167)
B. one or two (go to page 168)
C. none (go to page 169)

Heart, head, and life

The last detail we will examine on your hand is the relationship between your heart line, head line, and life line. You have indicated that your heart line intersects both your head line and your life line.

This is a very unsettling discovery. This indicates that you are exceedingly irritable, changeable in affections, constantly seeking excitement, and difficult to get along with. Your relationships will suffer if your attitude fails to change. Don't let this discovery influence you. You need to make the best of the situation.

Do you have any lines on the side of your hand below your pinky?

INSTRUCTIONS: If you make a loose fist and look at the side of your hand between your pinky finger and your heart line you may notice some lines. These lines of affection are usually easily found, but on some rare occasions they may be completely missing.

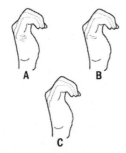

HINT: Make a fist and examine the side of your hand.

A. three or more (go to page 167)
B. one or two (go to page 168)
C. none (go to page 169)

Heart line by itself

It's nice to see that your heart line does not appear to intersect with your head line or life line. Keep in mind this could change with time. If your heart line begins to migrate to your head line it will be a reflection of possible turmoil in your relationships.

Keep a close eye on your heart line, in particular when you have entered into new relationships. Your heart line's behavior can change in just a matter of months.

Now let's continue with your reading. . .

Do you have any lines on the side of your hand below your pinky?

INSTRUCTIONS: If you make a loose fist and look at the side of your hand between your pinky finger and your heart line you may notice some lines. These lines of affection are usually easily found, but on some rare occasions they may be completely missing.

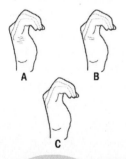

HINT: Make a fist and examine the side of your hand.

A. three or more (go to page 167)
B. one or two (go to page 168)
C. none (go to page 169)

Your heart's from Jupiter!

Now we can examine the starting point of your heart line. Since your heart line rises from the mount of Jupiter (below the index finger) you are extremely sentimental. Love is critical to your happiness.

You believe in the power of love. You would rather live in poverty with love, than with riches and an empty heart. You have a pure heart and a true understanding for compassion and commitment.

Let's continue your reading. . .

Where does your heart line end?

INSTRUCTIONS: Your heart line should travel from someplace near your index finger toward the other side of your hand. Heart lines end in different places on everybody's hands.

HINT: Follow your heart line to the end.

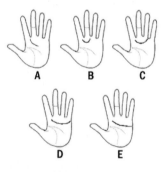

A. middle of the hand (go to page 182)
B. below the middle finger (go to page 184)
C. below the ring finger (go to page 186)
D. below the pinky finger (go to page 188)
E. other side of the palm (go to page 190)

Your heart's between your fingers!

Now we can examine the starting point of your heart line. Since your heart line rises between the mounts of Jupiter and Saturn (the index finger and middle finger) you fall in a "middle-ground" when it comes to affection. You are not carried away with sentiment and you view love from a practical standpoint.

You have a difficult time believing that a relationship can survive on love alone. You think that love in a cottage without plenty of bread and butter is a myth. You may be strong in affection, but you are not "foolish."

Let's continue your reading. . .

Where does your heart line end?

INSTRUCTIONS: Your heart line should travel from someplace near your index finger toward the other side of your hand. Heart lines end in different places on everybody's hands.

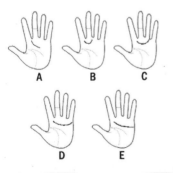

HINT: Follow your heart line to the end.

A. middle of the hand (go to page 182)
B. below the middle finger (go to page 184)
C. below the ring finger (go to page 186)
D. below the pinky finger (go to page 188)
E. other side of the palm (go to page 190)

Your heart rises from Saturn!

Now we can examine the starting point of your heart line. Since your heart line rises from the mount of Saturn (below the middle finger) you are a sensualist. While you may not be as sensual as your Apollo friends, you still have your own strong sensual desires.

Love coupled with a strong attraction will set your heart and mind on fire. You live for personal satisfaction. You are consumed with your senses.

Let's continue your reading. . .

Where does your heart line end?

INSTRUCTIONS: Your heart line should travel from someplace near your index finger toward the other side of your hand. Heart lines end in different places on everybody's hands.

HINT: Follow your heart line to the end.

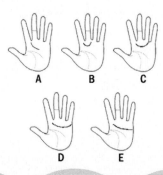

A. middle of the hand (go to page 182)
B. below the middle finger (go to page 184)
C. below the ring finger (go to page 186)
D. below the pinky finger (go to page 188)
E. other side of the palm (go to page 190)

Your heart's between your fingers!
Since your heart line rises from the mounts of both Jupiter and Saturn your heart represents the union of sentiment, common sense, and passion. You are a kind person with a warm heart.

You love your friends, all relationships, and humankind in general. Unfortunately, people have a habit of taking advantage of your charitable, loving attitude. You rarely look after your own interests when considering the interests of others. This selflessness is a great quality as long as you have great friends.

Where does your heart line end?

INSTRUCTIONS: Your heart line should travel from someplace near your index finger toward the other side of your hand. Heart lines end in different places on everybody's hands.

HINT: Follow your heart line to the end.

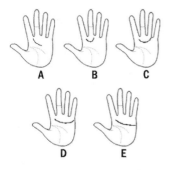

A. middle of the hand (go to page 182)
B. below the middle finger (go to page 184)
C. below the ring finger (go to page 186)
D. below the pinky finger (go to page 188)
E. other side of the palm (go to page 190)

Lots of space between your first two fingers

Since your Jupiter finger and Saturn finger have the most significant gap between them, you possess great independence of thought and you are not easily influenced by others. You form your own opinions. This makes you stubborn and may cause conflict in your relationships, especially if your partner shares this same quality.

Let's continue your reading. . .

How would you describe the shading of your hand?

INSTRUCTIONS: Your hand could have just about any shading to it. Hold your hand flat and look to see if you have a tinge of color in your palm. Look at your entire palm and determine what the general shading is.

HINT: Use the shades below as a reference.

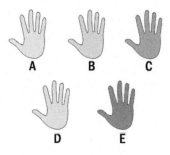

A. pale (go to page 133)
B. pink (go to page 134)
C. red (go to page 135)
D. yellow (go to page 136)
E. blue (go to page 137)

Na-Noo Na-Noo! (a la Mork from Ork)
Since your Saturn and Apollo fingers are well separated, you are careless with your future. You are Bohemian in thought and you are entirely devoid of stiffness and formality. You look for a partner that shares your ideas and nontraditional values.

Let's continue your reading. . .

How would you describe the shading of your hand?
INSTRUCTIONS: Your hand could have just about any shading to it. Hold your hand flat and look to see if you have a tinge of color in your palm. Look at your entire palm and determine what the general shading is.

HINT: Use the shades below as a reference.

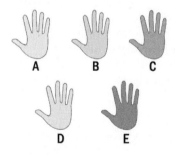

A. pale (go to page 133)
B. pink (go to page 134)
C. red (go to page 135)
D. yellow (go to page 136)
E. blue (go to page 137)

Lots of space between your ring and pinky fingers
Since your Apollo and Mercury fingers are well separated you are independent in action. You do whatever you please without any regard for what others may think. At times, your lack of consideration may cause tension between you and your partner.

Let's continue your reading. . .

How would you describe the shading of your hand?

INSTRUCTIONS: Your hand could have just about any shading to it. Hold your hand flat and look to see if you have a tinge of color in your palm. Look at your entire palm and determine what the general shading is.

HINT: Use the shades below as a reference.

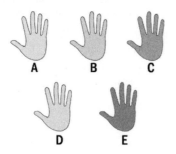

A. pale (go to page 133)
B. pink (go to page 134)
C. red (go to page 135)
D. yellow (go to page 136)
E. blue (go to page 137)

Lookin' pale

Finally let's discuss the coloring of your hand. Physiologically considered, blood, which produces color, performs two important functions. It swiftly travels through your veins and arteries and carries away impurities, and at the same time renews and sustains life.

You have described your hand as pale in color. At times you tend to be cold and distant, although this is not typical of the Martian type. You are uninterested in going out of your way to keep others happy. In your relationships you are unemotional and often selfish. You may need to make a more concerted effort to keep those you're closest to satisfied.

Your reading is complete!

In just minutes we have revealed valuable secrets concealed in your hand's unique characteristics. We've determined you are a Martian and–selfish tendencies aside–ultimately your romantic partner will be the beneficiary of undying passion. Your willingness to stand up for your lover will lead to relationships built on a foundation of commitment and desire.

Pink in the palms

Now let's discuss the coloring of your hand. Physiologically considered, blood, which produces color, performs two important functions. It swiftly travels through your veins and arteries and carries away impurities, and at the same time renews and sustains life.

The pink color of your hand indicates that a normal amount of blood is passing through your body. Consequently, you are robust and healthy, which is typical of the Martian prototype. In addition you are bright, cheerful, balanced, and vivacious. People are naturally attracted to you. You are tender, sympathetic, and you appreciate the power of love.

Your reading is complete!

In just minutes we have revealed valuable secrets concealed in your hand's unique characteristics. We've determined you are a Martian and ultimately your romantic partner will be the beneficiary of undying passion. Your willingness to stand up for your lover will lead to relationships built on a foundation of commitment and desire.

Caught red-handed!

Now let's discuss the coloring of your hand. Physiologically considered, blood, which produces color, performs two important functions. It swiftly travels through your veins and arteries and carries away impurities, and at the same time renews and sustains life.

Your red hands indicate rich blood, a strong heart, and much vitality, all of which are typical of the Martian type. When you love it is not with a feeble flame, but rather an overpowering blast of strength. Subsequently your relationships are intense and you periodically find yourself at odds with those you love.

Your reading is complete!

In just minutes we have revealed valuable secrets concealed in your hand's unique characteristics. We've determined you are a Martian and ultimately your romantic partner will be the beneficiary of undying passion. Your willingness to stand up for your lover will lead to relationships built on a foundation of commitment and desire.

Simply yellow

Now let's discuss the coloring of your hand. Physiologically considered, blood, which produces color, performs two important functions. It swiftly travels through your veins and arteries and carries away impurities, and at the same time renews and sustains life.

The yellow coloring of your hand indicates that you are moody, melancholy, and you often take a dark view of life. Although this is not typical of the Martian type, far too often you have "the blues."

Your reading is complete!

In just minutes we have revealed valuable secrets concealed in your hand's unique characteristics. We've determined you are a Martian and–melancholy tendencies aside–ultimately your romantic partner will be the beneficiary of undying passion. Your willingness to stand up for your lover will lead to relationships built on a foundation of commitment and desire.

Got the blues in your hands

Now let's discuss the coloring of your hand. Physiologically considered, blood, which produces color, performs two important functions. It swiftly travels through your veins and arteries and carries away impurities, and at the same time renews and sustains life.

The blue coloring of your hand indicates that your blood is not flowing very freely at the moment. You may have an unhealthy amount of stress. Take some time for yourself and don't get depressed when you hit bumps in the road.

Your reading is complete!

In just minutes we have revealed valuable secrets concealed in your hand's unique characteristics. We've determined you are a Martian and ultimately your romantic partner will be the beneficiary of undying passion. Your willingness to stand up for your lover will lead to relationships built on a foundation of commitment and desire.

Soft and smooth

Your soft hands indicate that you may have a tendency to be lazy, although this is not common among Jupiterians. This lack of energy demonstrated in your hand is reflected in how you deal with others. You may need to make an extra effort in order to maintain satisfying relationships.

How long is your thumb?

INSTRUCTIONS: This question is in reference to the length of your thumb. Hold your thumb flat against the side of your hand to see where the tip of your thumb meets your index finger.

HINT: Hold your thumb against the side of your hand and imagine a line traveling across your fingers from the top of your thumb.

A. short (go to page 175)
B. medium (go to page 177)
C. long (go to page 179)

A   B   C

Springy
The elasticity of your hands reflects your vigor and motivation. Your energy is well directed and everyone around you benefits from your positive attitude. You are trustworthy and you always take responsibility for your actions, as is common among Jupiterians.

How long is your thumb?

INSTRUCTIONS: This question is in reference to the length of your thumb. Hold your thumb flat against the side of your hand to see where the tip of your thumb meets your index finger.

HINT: Hold your thumb against the side of your hand and imagine a line traveling across your fingers from the top of your thumb.

A. short (go to page 175)
B. medium (go to page 177)
C. long (go to page 179)

Rough handed

Your coarse hands reflect your comfort with physical labor. Those around you are impressed by your physical strength and your desire to move mountains, which you can attribute to your Jupiterian influence. You appear to be uninterested in socializing with those who "think they're smart." You are easy to talk to and you appreciate simplicity.

How long is your thumb?

INSTRUCTIONS: This question is in reference to the length of your thumb. Hold your thumb flat against the side of your hand to see where the tip of your thumb meets your index finger.

HINT: Hold your thumb against the side of your hand and imagine a line traveling across your fingers from the top of your thumb.

A. short (go to page 175)
B. medium (go to page 177)
C. long (go to page 179)

A   B   C

Three's a crowd?

Your affection lines appear on the side of your hand between your pinky finger and your heart line. It appears that you have several lines of affection. You live an exciting love life. You are always on the move and it's not likely that you'll be settling down anytime soon.

You often become bored with long-term relationships and you appear to have an easy time moving on to something new. You may play the role of a committed lover, but those who know you well will see right through the facade.

How long is your thumb?

INSTRUCTIONS: This question is in reference to the length of your thumb. Hold your thumb flat against the side of your hand to see where the tip of your thumb meets your index finger.

HINT: Hold your thumb against the side of your hand and imagine a line traveling across your fingers from the top of your thumb.

A. short (go to page 175)
B. medium (go to page 177)
C. long (go to page 179)

One or two lines

Your affection lines appear on the side of your hand between your pinky finger and your heart line. It appears that you only have a few affection lines.

Although you've had some significant relationships you are more interested in finding one person to settle down with. You are uninterested in chasing after part-time lovers. You're looking for a rewarding relationship with someone who is as committed as you.

How long is your thumb?

INSTRUCTIONS: This question is in reference to the length of your thumb. Hold your thumb flat against the side of your hand to see where the tip of your thumb meets your index finger.

HINT: Hold your thumb against the side of your hand and imagine a line traveling across your fingers from the top of your thumb.

A B C

A. short (go to page 175)
B. medium (go to page 177)
C. long (go to page 179)

Limited affection lines

The last feature on your hand we will examine is your lines of affection. Your affection lines appear on the side of your hand between your pinky finger and your heart line. You have indicated that you don't have any affection lines. If the rest of your hand indicates a lack of affection this would only reinforce those discoveries.

Don't worry too much about this discovery. As you become more affectionate you will develop several lines of affection on the side of your hand. If you have a good heart these lines will develop in no time. Most likely these lines will appear as you grow older and you have experienced all the emotions tied to love.

How long is your thumb?

INSTRUCTIONS: This question is in reference to the length of your thumb. Hold your thumb flat against the side of your hand to see where the tip of your thumb meets your index finger.

A B C

HINT: Hold your thumb against the side of your hand and imagine a line traveling across your fingers from the top of your thumb.

A. short (go to page 175)
B. medium (go to page 177)
C. long (go to page 179)

A *chained heart*

The effect of the chained lines on your hand is the weak operation of the qualities of the line. If chains are seen on only part of a line, the weak, poor operation of the line will occur. The chains make it impossible for your current to flow freely and evenly through the line, creating a labored, strained, obstructed condition.

If the chain appears on your heart line you may be more sentimental than those around you. You may also have a tendency to become nervous and uncomfortable in risky relationships.

Let's continue your reading. . .

Which picture best represents the flexibility of your thumb?

INSTRUCTIONS: Hold your thumb in the air and bend the tip of your thumb back without any assistance from your other hand.

HINT: You are only determining the flexibility of the tip of your thumb.

A. stiff (go to page 187)
B. flexible (go to page 189)

A   B

Islands of the heart

The island formation on the lines of your hand divides the strength of the current, producing a consequent division of strength and force thus lessening their vital force. If you find significant islands on your heart line you will face some challenging times in your love life.

Let's continue your reading. . .

Which picture best represents the flexibility of your thumb?

INSTRUCTIONS: Hold your thumb in the air and bend the tip of your thumb back without any assistance from your other hand.

HINT: You are only determining the flexibility of the tip of your thumb.

A. stiff (go to page 187)
B. flexible (go to page 189)

A crossed heart

The crossed lines that appear on your heart line are a common sign. A deep-cut cross is a sign of grave importance, especially if highly colored. The cross is an obstacle or a defect, and can produce a bad quality or a change in the course of your love life.

Imagine the current of love running through your heart line. When your heart line crosses another line the strength of the line is diminished. Subsequently your heart line reflects a dwindling passion.

Let's continue your reading. . .

Which picture best represents the flexibility of your thumb?

INSTRUCTIONS: Hold your thumb in the air and bend the tip of your thumb back without any assistance from your other hand.

HINT: You are only determining the flexibility of the tip of your thumb.

A. stiff (go to page 187)
B. flexible (go to page 189)

A   B

A broken heart line

The breaks in the lines on your hand are frequently encountered and often indicate a defective condition. It signifies that the current is interrupted and stopped in exactly the same manner as when a telephone wire is cut. In some cases, the lines may eventually grow together or the current may jump over the break.

The wider the break, the more serious it becomes and the less likelihood there is of the current's passing over the space between the broken ends. The effects of this may be felt in your love life if the breaks are on the heart line and your head line.

Let's continue your reading. . .

Which picture best represents the flexibility of your thumb?

INSTRUCTIONS: Hold your thumb in the air and bend the tip of your thumb back without any assistance from your other hand.

HINT: You are only determining the flexibility of the tip of your thumb.

A. stiff (go to page 187)
B. flexible (go to page 189)

A   B

Your heart comes from Jupiter!
Since your heart line rises from the mount of Jupiter (below the index fin-ger) you are extremely sentimental. Love is critical to your happiness. You believe in the power of love. You would rather live in poverty with love, than with riches and an empty heart. You have a pure heart and a true understanding for compassion and commitment.

Let's continue your reading. . .

Which picture best represents the flexibility of your thumb?

INSTRUCTIONS: Hold your thumb in the air and bend the tip of your thumb back without any assistance from your other hand.

HINT: You are only determining the flexibility of the tip of your thumb.

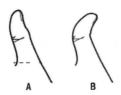

A. stiff (go to page 187)
B. flexible (go to page 189)

Your heart's between your fingers!

Now we can examine the starting point of your heart line. Since your heart line rises between the mounts of Jupiter and Saturn (the index finger and middle finger) you fall in a "middle-ground" when it comes to affection.

You are not carried away with sentiment and you view love from a practical standpoint. You have a difficult time believing that a relationship can survive on love alone. You think that love in a cottage without plenty of bread and butter is a myth. You may be strong in affection, but you are not "foolish."

Let's continue your reading. . .

Which picture best represents the flexibility of your thumb?

INSTRUCTIONS: Hold your thumb in the air and bend the tip of your thumb back without any assistance from your other hand.

HINT: You are only determining the flexibility of the tip of your thumb.

A. stiff (go to page 187)
B. flexible (go to page 189)

A   B

Your heart rises from Saturn

Now we can examine the starting point of your heart line. Since your heart line rises from the mount of Saturn (below the middle finger) you are a sensualist.

While you may not be as sensual as your Apollo friends, you still have your own strong sensual desires. Love coupled with a strong attraction will set your heart and mind on fire. You live for personal satisfaction. You are consumed with your senses.

Let's continue your reading. . .

Which picture best represents the flexibility of your thumb?

INSTRUCTIONS: Hold your thumb in the air and bend the tip of your thumb back without any assistance from your other hand.

HINT: You are only determining the flexibility of the tip of your thumb.

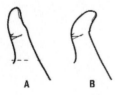

A. stiff (go to page 187)
B. flexible (go to page 189)

Your heart's between your fingers!

Now we can examine the starting point of your heart line. Since your heart line rises from the mounts of both Jupiter and Saturn your heart represents the union of sentiment, common sense, and passion. You are a kind person with a warm heart.

You love your friends, all relationships, and mankind in general. Unfortunately, people have a habit of taking advantage of your charitable, loving attitude. You rarely look after your own interests when considering the interests of others. This selflessness is a great quality as long as you have great friends.

Let's continue your reading. . .

Which picture best represents the flexibility of your thumb?

INSTRUCTIONS: Hold your thumb in the air and bend the tip of your thumb back without any assistance from your other hand.

HINT: You are only determining the flexibility of the tip of your thumb.

A. stiff (go to page 187)
B. flexible (go to page 189)

A   B

Your heart curves toward Saturn!

Upon closer examination of your heart line it appears as if you may be more influenced by Saturn than first thought. Your heart line shows a slight curve toward your middle finger indicating that the mount of Saturn may have a significant influence over you.

This is not a strong indication, but it should not be ignored. Once again if this is the case you may be feeling distant from those you have always loved and frustrated with life in general. Keep your chin up.

Do you have any lines on the side of your hand below your pinky?

INSTRUCTIONS: If you make a loose fist and look at the side of your hand between your pinky finger and your heart line you may notice some lines. These lines of affection are usually easily found, but on some rare occasions they may be completely missing.

HINT: Make a fist and examine the side of your hand.

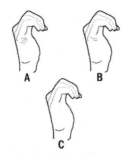

A. three or more (go to page 181)
B. one or two (go to page 183)
C. none (go to page 185)

Your heart line curves toward Apollo

Your heart line shows a slight curve toward your ring finger, simply another example of how the mount of Apollo may have a significant influence over you. This saturated influence may reflect your tendency to fall in love with beauty rather than character.

Physical attraction may take precedence over everything else. Someone with a strong influence from Apollo will care very little about personality.

Do you have any lines on the side of your hand below your pinky?

INSTRUCTIONS: If you make a loose fist and look at the side of your hand between your pinky finger and your heart line you may notice some lines. These lines of affection are usually easily found, but on some rare occasions they may be completely missing.

HINT: Make a fist and examine the side of your hand.

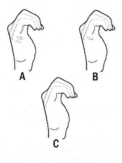

A. three or more (go to page 181)
B. one or two (go to page 183)
C. none (go to page 185)

Curving toward the pinky

Your heart line shows a slight curve toward your pinky finger indicating that the mount of Mercury may have a significant influence over you.

While this may not be a strong indication, it should not be ignored. If Mercury continues to have an influence you will become shrewd and significantly influenced by your finances. You will make decisions based on practicality and those around you may be turned off by your lack of sympathy.

Do you have any lines on the side of your hand below your pinky?

INSTRUCTIONS: If you make a loose fist and look at the side of your hand between your pinky finger and your heart line you may notice some lines. These lines of affection are usually easily found, but on some rare occasions they may be completely missing.

HINT: Make a fist and examine the side of your hand.

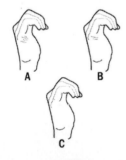

A. three or more (go to page 181)
B. one or two (go to page 183)
C. none (go to page 185)

A *straight heart line*

Upon closer examination of your heart line it appears as if the four major mounts at the top of your palm don't even have an influence on the behavior of your life line. You are balanced and you will not be swayed by the influences of others.

It's likely that your love life will be as even-keeled as your heart line. You may not have the most interesting relationships, but you will surely have the most rewarding.

Do you have any lines on the side of your hand below your pinky?

INSTRUCTIONS: If you make a loose fist and look at the side of your hand between your pinky finger and your heart line you may notice some lines. These lines of affection are usually easily found, but on some rare occasions they may be completely missing.

HINT: Make a fist and examine the side of your hand.

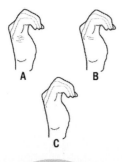

A. three or more (go to page 181)
B. one or two (go to page 183)
C. none (go to page 185)

Your heart stops in the middle

We continue our reading of the heart line by examining the length of the line as well as the location on your hand where the heart line terminates. Your heart line ends close to the middle of your hand.

The length of your heart line indicates that while you are loving, you are also practical. You make wise, confident decisions related to love. You are ready for just about anything and you welcome the emotions that come with a strong relationship.

Do you have any lines on the side of your hand below your pinky?

INSTRUCTIONS: If you make a loose fist and look at the side of your hand between your pinky finger and your heart line you may notice some lines. These lines of affection are usually easily found, but on some rare occasions they may be completely missing.

HINT: Make a fist and examine the side of your hand.

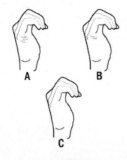

A. three or more (go to page 181)
B. one or two (go to page 183)
C. none (go to page 185)

Heart-stopping Saturn

It's important to examine the termination of your heart line. Your heart line terminates close to the mount of Saturn below your middle finger.

This means several things. Since your heart line is quite short you are usually a bit cold and "heartless." You were born with a good heart, but time has had an impact on your affection. In addition, since your heart line ends below your middle finger, Saturnian qualities are beginning to take control of your heart. Most noticeable are the Saturnian's indifference and lack of emotion.

Do you have any lines on the side of your hand below your pinky?

INSTRUCTIONS: If you make a loose fist and look at the side of your hand between your pinky finger and your heart line you may notice some lines. These lines of affection are usually easily found, but on some rare occasions they may be completely missing.

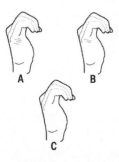

HINT: Make a fist and examine the side of your hand.

A. three or more (go to page 181)
B. one or two (go to page 183)
C. none (go to page 185)

Your heart line stops below your ring finger
Your heart line terminates close to the mount of Apollo, just below your ring finger. You are attracted to the Apollonian ideas of beauty and art.

You are consumed with beauty and in marriage you are likely to be unhappy unless you find someone with your same ideals. Your ideal mate will have a heart line that behaves much like yours.

Do you have any lines on the side of your hand below your pinky?

INSTRUCTIONS: If you make a loose fist and look at the side of your hand between your pinky finger and your heart line you may notice some lines. These lines of affection are usually easily found, but on some rare occasions they may be completely missing.

HINT: Make a fist and examine the side of your hand.

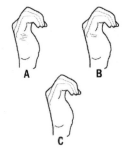

A. three or more (go to page 181)
B. one or two (go to page 183)
C. none (go to page 185)

Your heart goes to your pinky

Your heart line terminates close to the mount of Mercury, just below your pinky finger. This means that finances largely influence your affections.

The Mercurian shrewdness guides this heart line; therefore money must always be in sight before love is recognized. When you love your love is strong, but you don't act on impulsive affection.

Do you have any lines on the side of your hand below your pinky?

INSTRUCTIONS: If you make a loose fist and look at the side of your hand between your pinky finger and your heart line you may notice some lines. These lines of affection are usually easily found, but on some rare occasions they may be completely missing.

HINT: Make a fist and examine the side of your hand.

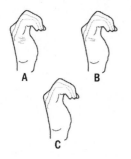

A. three or more (go to page 181)
B. one or two (go to page 183)
C. none (go to page 185)

Your heart goes all the way

Your heart line terminates all the way on the other side of your palm. You bring a new meaning to the word affection. You have too much heart and you allow sentiment to guide you in everything.

You easily become jealous and you will suffer if the love you share with others is not returned. Some palmists have read this line as a sign that you will "fail in all enterprises" because you have too much compassion. This is not accurate. You simply need to be more careful about sharing your compassion only with those who really deserve it.

Do you have any lines on the side of your hand below your pinky?

INSTRUCTIONS: If you make a loose fist and look at the side of your hand between your pinky finger and your heart line you may notice some lines. These lines of affection are usually easily found, but on some rare occasions they may be completely missing.

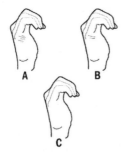

HINT: Make a fist and examine the side of your hand.

A. three or more (go to page 181)
B. one or two (go to page 183)
C. none (go to page 185)

Think thick

You need not be too concerned with the base of your finger being thick. If the base of your finger is extremely thick you should be wary of a growing desire for luxury. Your desire to have the best of everything may lead you down a path of deceit and significantly affect your relationships.

How long is your thumb?

INSTRUCTIONS: This question is in reference to the length of your thumb. Hold your thumb flat against the side of your hand to see where the tip of your thumb meets your index finger.

HINT: Hold your thumb against the side of your hand and imagine a line traveling across your fingers from the top of your thumb.

A. short (go to page 176)
B. medium (go to page 178)
C. long (go to page 180)

Here's the skinny

Since the base of your finger is "waist-like" you expend your energy in the mental and business worlds, rather than the sensual. Your extreme curiosity may have an impact on all of those with whom you associate. Be careful not to pry, because it may cause you more pain than pleasure. Take control of your curiosity.

How long is your thumb?

INSTRUCTIONS: This question is in reference to the length of your thumb. Hold your thumb flat against the side of your hand to see where the tip of your thumb meets your index finger.

HINT: Hold your thumb against the side of your hand and imagine a line traveling across your fingers from the top of your thumb.

A. short (go to page 176)
B. medium (go to page 178)
C. long (go to page 180)

A   B   C

A *chained love*

The effect of the chained heart line on your hand is the weak operation of the qualities of the line. If chains are seen on only part of a line, the weak, poor operation of the line will occur.

The chains make it impossible for your current to flow freely and evenly through the line, creating a labored, strained, obstructed condition. If the chain appears on your heart line you may be more sentimental than those around you. You may also have a tendency to become nervous and uncomfortable in risky relationships.

How long is your thumb?

INSTRUCTIONS: This question is in reference to the length of your thumb. Hold your thumb flat against the side of your hand to see where the tip of your thumb meets your index finger.

HINT: Hold your thumb against the side of your hand and imagine a line traveling across your fingers from the top of your thumb.

A. short (go to page 176)
B. medium (go to page 178)
C. long (go to page 180)

A   B   C

An island of love

The island formation on the lines of your hand divides the strength of the current, producing a consequent division of strength and force thus lessening their vital force.

If you find significant islands on your heart line you will face some challenging times in your love life.

How long is your thumb?

INSTRUCTIONS: This question is in reference to the length of your thumb. Hold your thumb flat against the side of your hand to see where the tip of your thumb meets your index finger.

HINT: Hold your thumb against the side of your hand and imagine a line traveling across your fingers from the top of your thumb.

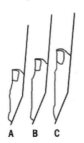

A. short (go to page 176)
B. medium (go to page 178)
C. long (go to page 180)

A   B   C

A crossed heart

The crossed lines that appear on your heart line are a common sign. A deep-cut cross is a sign of grave importance, especially if highly colored. The cross is an obstacle or a defect, and can produce a bad quality or a change in the course of your love life.

Imagine the current of love running through your heart line. When your heart line crosses another line the strength of the line is diminished. Subsequently your heart line reflects a dwindling passion.

How long is your thumb?

INSTRUCTIONS: This question is in reference to the length of your thumb. Hold your thumb flat against the side of your hand to see where the tip of your thumb meets your index finger.

HINT: Hold your thumb against the side of your hand and imagine a line traveling across your fingers from the top of your thumb.

A. short (go to page 176)
B. medium (go to page 178)
C. long (go to page 180)

A B C

A broken heart?

The breaks in your heart line frequently indicate a defective condition. It signifies that the current is interrupted and stopped in exactly the same manner as when a telephone wire is cut. In some cases, the lines may eventually grow together or the current may jump over the break.

The wider the break, the more serious it becomes and the less likelihood there is of the current's passing over the space between the broken ends. The effects of this may be felt in your love life if the breaks are on the heart line and your head line.

How long is your thumb?

INSTRUCTIONS: This question is in reference to the length of your thumb. Hold your thumb flat against the side of your hand to see where the tip of your thumb meets your index finger.

HINT: Hold your thumb against the side of your hand and imagine a line traveling across your fingers from the top of your thumb.

A. short (go to page 176)
B. medium (go to page 178)
C. long (go to page 180)

Lots of affection lines

Your affection lines appear on the side of your hand between your pinky finger and your heart line. It appears that you have several lines of affection. You live an exciting love life. You are always on the move and it's not likely that you'll be settling down anytime soon.

You often become bored with long-term relationships and you appear to have an easy time moving on to something new. You may play the role of a committed lover, but those who know you well will see right through the facade.

How long is your thumb?

INSTRUCTIONS: This question is in reference to the length of your thumb. Hold your thumb flat against the side of your hand to see where the tip of your thumb meets your index finger.

HINT: Hold your thumb against the side of your hand and imagine a line traveling across your fingers from the top of your thumb.

A. short (go to page 191)
B. medium (go to page 192)
C. long (go to page 193)

A   B   C

One or two lines

Your affection lines appear on the side of your hand between your pinky finger and your heart line. It appears that you only have a few affection lines.

Although you've had some significant relationships you are more interested in finding one person to settle down with. You are uninterested in chasing after part-time lovers. You're looking for a rewarding relationship with someone who is as committed as you.

How long is your thumb?

INSTRUCTIONS: This question is in reference to the length of your thumb. Hold your thumb flat against the side of your hand to see where the tip of your thumb meets your index finger.

HINT: Hold your thumb against the side of your hand and imagine a line traveling across your fingers from the top of your thumb.

A. short (go to page 191)
B. medium (go to page 192)
C. long (go to page 193)

A   B   C

Limited affection lines

Your affection lines appear on the side of your hand between your pinky finger and your heart line. You have indicated that you don't have any affection lines. If the rest of your hand indicates a lack of affection this would only reinforce those discoveries.

Don't worry too much about this discovery. As you become more affectionate you will develop several lines of affection on the side of your hand. If you have a good heart these lines will develop in no time. Most likely these lines will appear as you grow older and you have experienced all the emotions tied to love.

How long is your thumb?

INSTRUCTIONS: This question is in reference to the length of your thumb. Hold your thumb flat against the side of your hand to see where the tip of your thumb meets your index finger.

HINT: Hold your thumb against the side of your hand and imagine a line traveling across your fingers from the top of your thumb.

A. short (go to page 191)
B. medium (go to page 192)
C. long (go to page 193)

A   B   C

Straight to the middle

Your heart line ends close to the middle of your hand. This is interesting, since your heart line is not strongly influenced by any of the major mounts. The length of your heart line indicates that while you are loving, you are also practical.

You make wise, confident decisions related to love. You are ready for just about anything and you welcome the emotions that come with a strong relationship.

How long is your thumb?

INSTRUCTIONS: This question is in reference to the length of your thumb. Hold your thumb flat against the side of your hand to see where the tip of your thumb meets your index finger.

HINT: Hold your thumb against the side of your hand and imagine a line traveling across your fingers from the top of your thumb.

A. short (go to page 191)
B. medium (go to page 192)
C. long (go to page 193)

Your heart goes to Saturn!
Your heart line terminates close to the mount of Saturn below your middle finger. This means several things.

Since your heart line is quite short you are usually a bit cold and "heartless." You were born with a good heart, but time has had an impact on your affection. In addition, since your heart line ends below your middle finger Saturnian qualities are beginning to take control of your heart. Most noticeable are the Saturnian's lack of emotion and indifference.

How long is your thumb?

INSTRUCTIONS: This question is in reference to the length of your thumb. Hold your thumb flat against the side of your hand to see where the tip of your thumb meets your index finger.

HINT: Hold your thumb against the side of your hand and imagine a line traveling across your fingers from the top of your thumb.

A. B. C.

A. short (go to page 191)
B. medium (go to page 192)
C. long (go to page 193)

Your heart's going to Apollo!
We continue our reading of the heart line by examining the length of the line as well as the location on your hand where the heart line appears to terminate. Your heart line terminates close to the mount of Apollo, just below your ring finger.

You are attracted to the Apollonian ideas of beauty and art. You are consumed with beauty and in marriage you are likely to be unhappy unless you find someone with your same ideals. Your ideal mate will have a heart line that behaves much like yours.

How long is your thumb?

INSTRUCTIONS: This question is in reference to the length of your thumb. Hold your thumb flat against the side of your hand to see where the tip of your thumb meets your index finger.

HINT: Hold your thumb against the side of your hand and imagine a line traveling across your fingers from the top of your thumb.

A. short (go to page 191)
B. medium (go to page 192)
C. long (go to page 193)

A   B   C

Your heart goes to Mercury!

Your heart line terminates close to the mount of Mercury, just below your pinky finger. This means that finances largely influence your affections.

The Mercurian shrewdness guides this heart line; therefore money must always be in sight before love is recognized. When you love your love is strong, but you don't act on impulsive affection.

How long is your thumb?

INSTRUCTIONS: This question is in reference to the length of your thumb. Hold your thumb flat against the side of your hand to see where the tip of your thumb meets your index finger.

HINT: Hold your thumb against the side of your hand and imagine a line traveling across your fingers from the top of your thumb.

A. short (go to page 191)
B. medium (go to page 192)
C. long (go to page 193)

A   B   C

Your heart goes all the way to the other side

Your heart line terminates all the way on the other side of your palm. You bring a new meaning to the word affection. You have too much heart and you allow sentiment to guide you in everything. You easily become jealous and you will suffer if the love you share with others is not returned.

Some palmists have read this line as a sign that you will "fail in all enter-prises" because you have too much compassion. This is not accurate. You simply need to be more careful about sharing your compassion only with those who really deserve it.

How long is your thumb?

INSTRUCTIONS: This question is in reference to the length of your thumb. Hold your thumb flat against the side of your hand to see where the tip of your thumb meets your index finger.

HINT: Hold your thumb against the side of your hand and imagine a line traveling across your fingers from the top of your thumb.

A. short (go to page 191)
B. medium (go to page 192)
C. long (go to page 193)

A   B   C

Small thumb

Your small thumb demonstrates possible weakness in your character. Since your character may lack force you may find yourself having difficulty asserting your wants and needs to others and therefore may opt to stay in a potentially hazardous relationship.

Your reading is complete!

In just minutes we have revealed valuable secrets concealed in your hand's unique characteristics. We've determined you are a Jupiterian. Typically, relationships are controlled by Jupiterians, but during our last examination of your thumb we discovered that you may not be as controlling as other Jupiterians. Is your lover a Jupiterian?

Keep in mind that as time passes your hand's characteristics will also evolve. Lines may grow longer, thumbs may become more flexible, and the coloring of the palm may evolve. If you are interested in your romantic growth you should be sure to read your palm periodically. Better yet, maybe it's time to read your lover's palm.

Small thumb

Your small thumb demonstrates possible weakness in your character. Since your character may lack force you may find yourself having difficulty asserting your wants and needs to others and therefore may opt to stay in a potentially hazardous relationship.

Your reading is complete!

In just minutes we have revealed valuable secrets concealed in your hand's unique characteristics. We've determined you are a Mercurian. Typically, Mercurians are excellent judges of human nature. You aren't likely to waste your time with an unfaithful lover. You should continue to maintain your high standards in your love life. It might be time to examine your lover's hand and see if you share these qualities.

Keep in mind that as time passes your hand's characteristics will also evolve. Lines may grow longer, thumbs may become more flexible, and the coloring of the palm may evolve. If you are interested in your romantic growth you should examine your palm periodically.

Medium thumb

You may find that you are controlled and influenced in romantic situations by those you encounter with large thumbs. You also may find yourself a strong and attractive mate to others whose thumbs are smaller than yours. Recognizing this duality, it will be important for you to realize what role you play in your romantic relationships to better understand and improve your dynamic with your mate.

Your reading is complete!

In just minutes we have revealed valuable secrets concealed in your hand's unique characteristics. We've determined you are a Jupiterian. Typically, relationships are controlled by Jupiterians, but during our last examination of your thumb we discovered that you may not always be the one in control.

Keep in mind that as time passes your hand's characteristics will also evolve. Lines may grow longer, thumbs may become more flexible, and the coloring of the palm may evolve. If you are interested in your growth you should examine your palm periodically.

Medium thumb

You may find that you are controlled and influenced in romantic situations by those you encounter with large thumbs. You also may find yourself a strong and attractive mate to others whose thumbs are smaller than yours.

Recognizing this duality, it will be important for you to realize what role you play in your romantic relationships to better understand and improve your dynamic with your mate.

Your reading is complete!

In just minutes we have revealed valuable secrets concealed in your hand's unique characteristics. We've determined you are a Mercurian. Typically, Mercurians are excellent judges of human nature. You aren't likely to waste your time with an unfaithful lover. You should continue to maintain your high standards in your love life. Be sure to examine your lover's palm and see if you share these qualities.

Keep in mind that as time passes your hand's characteristics will also evolve. Lines may grow longer, thumbs may become more flexible, and the coloring of the palm may evolve. If you are interested in your romantic growth you should examine your palm periodically.

Thumbs of power

Keep in mind that there are some negatives to having a powerful thumb. Those with large thumbs are generally not emotional or sentimental and this may cause friction in relationships. People with large thumbs are also lovers of history, are natural leaders, and enjoy practical pursuits.

Your reading is complete!

In just minutes we have revealed valuable secrets concealed in your hand's unique characteristics. We've determined you are a Jupiterian. Typically, relationships are controlled by Jupiterians, and our last examination of your thumb confirms this. You may want to examine your lover's hand to see if your desire for control will have a negative impact on your relationship.

Keep in mind that as time passes your hand's characteristics will also evolve. With love lost or even love found you should always consider the romantic information reflected in your hand. Over time lines may grow longer, thumbs may become more flexible, and the coloring of the palm may evolve. If you are interested in your romantic growth you should examine your palm periodically.

Thumbs of power

Keep in mind that there are some negatives to having a powerful thumb. Those with large thumbs are generally not emotional or sentimental and this may cause friction in relationships. People with large thumbs are also lovers of history, are natural leaders, and enjoy practical pursuits.

Your reading is complete!

In just minutes we have revealed valuable secrets concealed in your hand's unique characteristics. We've determined you are a Mercurian. Typically, Mercurians are excellent judges of human nature. In fact you aren't likely to waste your time with an unfaithful lover. The question becomes, does your lover share your high standards? Maybe it's time to examine your lover's hand.

Keep in mind that as time passes your hand's characteristics will also evolve. Lines may grow longer, thumbs may become more flexible, and the coloring of the palm may evolve. If you are interested in your romantic growth you should examine your palm periodically.

Lots of affection lines

Your affection lines appear on the side of your hand between your pinky finger and your heart line. It appears that you have several lines of affection. You live an exciting love life. You are always on the move and it's not likely that you'll be settling down anytime soon.

You often become bored with long-term relationships and you appear to have an easy time moving on to something new. You may play the role of a committed lover, but those who know you well will see right through the facade.

Your reading is complete!

In just minutes we have revealed valuable secrets concealed in your hand's unique characteristics. We've determined you are a Apollonian. Typically, Apollonians are lovers of beauty. It's not surprising to see that you surround yourself with everything beautiful. Hopefully your lover will live up to your standards. Maybe it's time to examine your lover's hand.

Keep in mind that as your love life evolves your hand's characteristics will also evolve. Lines may grow longer, thumbs may become more flexible, and the coloring of the palm may evolve. If you are interested in your romantic growth you should examine your palm periodically.

Heart in the middle

We complete our reading by examining the heart line and where it terminates. Your heart line ends close to the middle of your hand. This is interesting, since your heart line is not strongly influenced by any of the major mounts.

The length of your heart line indicates that while you are loving, you are also practical. You make wise, confident decisions related to love. You are ready for just about anything and you welcome the emotions that come with a strong relationship.

Your reading is complete!

In just minutes we have revealed valuable secrets concealed in your hand's unique characteristics. We've determined you are a Lunarian. Typically, Lunarians enjoy the most scandalous relationships. Ultimately you'll go out of your way to keep your love life private.

Keep in mind that as you find love and lose love your hand's characteristics will evolve. You may want to read your palm every few months. Better yet, you may want to read your lover's palm.

One or two affection lines

Your affection lines appear on the side of your hand between your pinky finger and your heart line. It appears that you only have a few affection lines.

This discovery indicates that although you've had some significant relationships you are more interested in finding one person to settle down with. You aren't interested in chasing after part-time lovers. You're looking for a rewarding relationship with someone who is as committed as you.

Your reading is complete!

In just minutes we have revealed valuable secrets concealed in your hand's unique characteristics. We've determined you are an Apollonian. Typically, Apollonians are lovers of beauty. It's not surprising to see that you surround yourself with everything beautiful. Hopefully your lover will live up to your standards.

Keep in mind that as time passes your hand's characteristics will also evolve. Lines may grow longer, thumbs may become more flexible, and the coloring of the palm may evolve. If you are interested in your romantic growth you should examine your palm periodically.

Your heart goes to Saturn!

We complete our reading by examining the heart line and where it terminates. Your heart line terminates close to the mount of Saturn below your
middle finger. This means several things. Since your heart line is quite short
you are usually a bit cold and "heartless." You were born with a good heart,
but time has had an impact on your affection.

In addition since your heart line ends below your middle finger Saturnian
qualities are beginning to take control of your heart. Most noticeable are the
Saturnian's lack of emotion and indifference. You could use a bit more passion!

Your reading is complete!

In just minutes we have revealed valuable secrets concealed in your hand's
unique characteristics. We've determined you are a Lunarian. Typically,
Lunarians enjoy the most scandalous relationships. Ultimately you'll go out
of your way to keep your love life private.

Keep in mind that as you find love and lose love your hand's characteristics
will evolve. Lines may grow longer, thumbs may become more flexible, and
the coloring of the palm may evolve. If you are interested in your romantic
growth you should examine your palm periodically. Better yet, maybe you
should take a look at your lover's hand.

Limited affection

Your affection lines appear on the side of your hand between your pinky finger and your heart line. You have indicated that you don't have any affection lines. If the rest of your hand indicates a lack of affection this would only reinforce those discoveries.

Don't worry too much about this discovery. As you become more affectionate you will develop several lines of affection on the side of your hand. If you have a good heart these lines will develop in no time. Most likely these lines will appear as you grow older and you have experienced all the emotions tied to love.

Your reading is complete!

In just minutes we have revealed valuable secrets concealed in your hand's unique characteristics. We've determined you are an Apollonian. Typically, Apollonians are lovers of beauty. It's not surprising to see that you surround yourself with everything beautiful. Hopefully your lover will live up to your standards.

Keep in mind that as time passes your hand's characteristics will also evolve. Lines may grow longer, thumbs may become more flexible, and the coloring of the palm may evolve. If you are interested in your romantic growth you should examine your palm periodically.

Your heart goes to Apollo!

We complete our reading by examining the heart line and where it terminates. Your heart line terminates close to the mount of Apollo, just below your ring finger.

It's not surprising to see that you are attracted to the Apollonian ideas of beauty and art. You are consumed with beauty and in marriage you are likely to be unhappy unless you find someone with your same ideals. Your ideal mate will have a heart line that behaves much like yours.

Your reading is complete!

In just minutes we have revealed valuable secrets concealed in your hand's unique characteristics. We've determined you are a Lunarian. Typically, Lunarians enter into the most intriguing relationships. Your friends may criticize your romantic approach, but you should live your life how you choose. Better yet, maybe it's time to examine your friends' palms.

Keep in mind that as you lose love and find love your hand's characteristics will also evolve. Lines may grow longer, thumbs may become more flexible, and the coloring of the palm may evolve. If you are interested in your growth you should examine your palm periodically.

Stiff thumb

Since your thumb is stiff, you are practical, economical, stingy, and weigh everything carefully. As is expected of a Saturnian, you possess a strong will, stubborn determination, and are cautious, reserved, and do not give or invite confidence.

You are steady, not extremist, do not expect a great deal, and are consequently not disappointed when you do not receive what you expect from others.

Your reading is complete!

In just minutes we have revealed valuable secrets concealed in your hand's unique characteristics. We've determined you are a Saturnian. Typically, Saturnians are prudent and wise. Ultimately you have high standards. Hopefully you will find a lover who can live up to your romantic standards. I think this would be your cue to read your lover's palm.

Keep in mind that as you lose love and find love your hand's characteristics will also evolve. Lines may grow longer, thumbs may become more flexible, and the coloring of the palm may evolve. If you are interested in your growth you should examine your palm periodically.

Your heart goes to Mercury!

We complete our reading by examining the heart line and where it terminates. As a Lunarian it's surprising to see that your heart line terminates close to the mount of Mercury, just below your pinky finger.

This discovery indicates that finances largely influence your affections. The Mercurian shrewdness guides this heart line; therefore money must always be in sight before love is recognized. When you love your love is strong, but you don't act on impulsive affection.

Your reading is complete!

In just minutes we have revealed valuable secrets concealed in your hand's unique characteristics. We've determined you are a Lunarian. Typically, Lunarians enjoy the most scandalous relationships. Ultimately you'll go out of your way to keep your love life private.

Keep in mind that as you lose love and find love your hand's characteristics will also evolve. Lines may grow longer, thumbs may become more flexible, and the coloring of the palm may evolve. If you are interested in your growth you should examine your palm periodically.

Bendy thumb

Since your thumb is supple and flexible, you are the personification of extravagance. This takes some of the strength from your Saturnian influence, making you brilliant, versatile, and easily adaptable to changing circumstances.

You are at home anywhere, are sentimental, generous, sympathetic, and will give your last cent to a beggar. You are emotional and, consequently, an extremist, up one day, in the depths the next. While your friends and family may appreciate your flexibility, they may find your mood swings difficult to bear.

Your reading is complete!

In just minutes we have revealed valuable secrets concealed in your hand's unique characteristics. We've determined you are a Saturnian. Typically, Saturnians are prudent and wise. Ultimately you have high standards. Hopefully you will find a lover who can live up to your romantic standards. This may be a good reason to read your lover's palm.

Keep in mind that as time passes your hand's characteristics will also evolve. Lines may grow longer, thumbs may become more flexible, and the coloring of the palm may evolve. If you are interested in your growth you should examine your palm periodically.

Your heart goes all the way

We complete our reading by examining the heart line and where it terminates. Your heart line terminates all the way on the other side of your palm. You bring a new meaning to the word affection. You have too much heart and you allow sentiment to guide you in everything.

You easily become jealous and you will suffer if the love you share with others is not returned. Some palmists have read this line as a sign that you will "fail in all enterprises" because you have too much compassion. This is not accurate. You simply need to be more careful about sharing your compassion only with those who really deserve it.

Your reading is complete!

In just minutes we have revealed valuable secrets concealed in your hand's unique characteristics. We've determined you are a Lunarian. Typically, Lunarians enter into the most intriguing relationships. Your friends may criticize your romantic approach, but you should live your life how you choose.

Keep in mind that as time passes your hand's characteristics will also evolve. Lines may grow longer, thumbs may become more flexible, and the coloring of the palm may evolve. If you are interested in your growth you should examine your palm periodically.

Stubby thumb

The size of your thumb indicates that you often have difficulty asserting your needs. If you don't recognize this weakness you may find yourself frustrated with the direction your love life is headed.

Your reading is complete!

In just minutes we have revealed valuable secrets concealed in your hand's unique characteristics. We've determined you are a Venusian. Typically, Venusians are passionate lovers. In fact at times you may need to conceal your passion. Sometimes it's better to let love come to you.

Keep in mind that as time passes your hand's characteristics will also evolve. Lines may grow longer, thumbs may become more flexible, and the coloring of the palm may evolve. If you are interested in your romantic growth you should examine your palm periodically.

Medium thumb

Your sensitive disposition attracts the affections of many. Your thumb shows an understanding and appreciation that most people lack. Hopefully this positive quality will rub off on those who come into your life.

Your reading is complete!

In just minutes we have revealed valuable secrets concealed in your hand's unique characteristics. We've determined you are a Venusian. Typically, Venusians are passionate lovers. In fact at times you may need to conceal your passion. Sometimes it's better to let love come to you.

If you prefer to seek out romance why not use this book as a tool? Approach your crush and ask your potential lover if you can conduct a palm reading. That's one way to break the ice!

Long thumb

Unlike most Venusians your thumb appears to indicate that you lack tact. You will do just about anything to get your way.

While some may find your actions to be selfish, it's merely a reflection of your strong will. While your willpower will help you overcome personal troubles, it may also leave some people feeling a bit intimidated.

Your reading is complete!

In just minutes we have revealed valuable secrets concealed in your hand's unique characteristics. We've determined you are a Venusian. Typically, Venusians are passionate lovers. In fact at times you may need to conceal your passion. Sometimes it's better to let love come to you.

If you prefer to seek out romance why not use this book as a tool? Approach your crush and ask your potential lover if you can conduct a palm reading. That's one way to break the ice!

Heart in the middle

We continue our reading of the heart line by examining the length of the line as well as the location on your hand where the heart line terminates. Your heart line ends close to the middle of your hand. This is interesting, since your heart line is not strongly influenced by any of the major mounts.

The length of your heart line indicates that while you are loving, you are also practical. You make wise, confident decisions related to love. You are ready for just about anything and you welcome the emotions that come with a strong relationship.

What color is your heart line?

INSTRUCTIONS: The heart line runs across the top of the palm. There is a wide range of heart line colors. It's up to you to determine which color below best describes your heart line.

HINT: Be sure to look at your palm under bright, natural light.

A. pale (go to page 90)
B. pink (go to page 91)
C. red (go to page 92)
D. yellow (go to page 93)
E. blue (go to page 94)

Your heart goes to Saturn!

We continue our reading of the heart line by examining the length of the line as well as the location on your hand where the heart line appears to terminate. Your heart line terminates close to the mount of Saturn below your middle finger. This means several things. Since your heart line is quite short some people find you a bit cold and sometimes "heartless."

You were born with a good heart, but time has had an impact on your affection. In addition, since your heart line ends below your middle finger Saturnian qualities are beginning to take control of your heart. Most noticeable are the Saturnian's lack of emotion and indifference.

What color is your heart line?

INSTRUCTIONS: The heart line runs across the top of the palm. There is a wide range of heart line colors. It's up to you to determine which color below best describes your heart line.

HINT: Be sure to look at your palm under bright, natural light.

A. pale (go to page 90)
B. pink (go to page 91)
C. red (go to page 92)
D. yellow (go to page 93)
E. blue (go to page 94)

Your heart goes to Apollo!

We continue our reading of the heart line by examining the length of the line as well as the location on your hand where the heart line appears to terminate. Your heart line terminates close to the mount of Apollo, just below your ring finger.

You are attracted to the Apollonian ideas of beauty and art. You are consumed with beauty and in marriage you are likely to be unhappy unless you find someone with your same ideals. Your ideal mate will have a heart line that behaves much like yours.

What color is your heart line?

Instructions: The heart line runs across the top of the palm. There is a wide range of heart line colors. It's up to you to determine which color below best describes your heart line.

Hint: Be sure to look at your palm under bright, natural light.

A. pale (go to page 90)
B. pink (go to page 91)
C. red (go to page 92)
D. yellow (go to page 93)
E. blue (go to page 94)

Your heart goes to Mercury!

We continue our reading of the heart line by examining the length of the line as well as the location on your hand where the heart line appears to terminate. Your heart line terminates close to the mount of Mercury, just below your pinky finger. This means that finances largely influence your affections.

The Mercurian shrewdness guides this heart line; therefore money must always be in sight before love is recognized. When you love your love is strong, but you don't act on impulsive affection.

What color is your heart line?

INSTRUCTIONS: The heart line runs across the top of the palm. There is a wide range of heart line colors. It's up to you to determine which color below best describes your heart line.

HINT: Be sure to look at your palm under bright, natural light.

A. pale (go to page 90)
B. pink (go to page 91)
C. red (go to page 92)
D. yellow (go to page 93)
E. blue (go to page 94)

Your heart line goes all the way

We continue our reading of the heart line by examining the length of the line as well as the location on your hand where the heart line appears to terminate. Your heart line terminates all the way on the opposite side of your palm. You bring a new meaning to the word affection. You have too much heart and you allow sentiment to guide you in everything.

You easily become jealous and you will suffer if the love you share with others is not returned. Some palmists have read this line as a sign that you will "fail in all enterprises" because you have too much compassion. This is not necessarily true. You simply need to be more careful about sharing your compassion only with those who really deserve it.

What color is your heart line?

INSTRUCTIONS: The heart line runs across the top of the palm. There is a wide range of heart line colors. It's up to you to determine which color below best describes your heart line.

HINT: Be sure to look at your palm under bright, natural light.

A. pale (go to page 90)
B. pink (go to page 91)
C. red (go to page 92)
D. yellow (go to page 93)
E. blue (go to page 94)

A *pale heart*

You may have a heart line, but its pale coloring may leave you feeling cold and lonely. You are certain to have trouble finding love, and even when you've found it you may struggle to keep it.

Don't surrender to the symbols and signs found on your hand. You control your own destiny. If you are serious about improving your love life just make the extra effort. Over time you'll notice that your pale lines will turn to pink!

Let's continue your reading. . .

Do you have any lines on the side of your hand below your pinky?

INSTRUCTIONS: If you make a loose fist and look at the side of your hand between your pinky finger and your heart line you may notice some lines. These lines of affection are usually easily found, but on some rare occasions they may be completely missing.

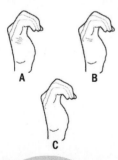

HINT: Make a fist and examine the side of your hand.

A. three or more (go to page 167)
B. one or two (go to page 168)
C. none (go to page 169)

Pretty in pink

Your pink heart line is a pleasant reward for being compassionate and warm. As long as your heart line retains this shading you are sure to be a true romantic.

You are unlikely to fall in love with someone who holds a pale heart line, but if you do it's certain that your affection will turn their heart line pink.

Let's continue your reading. . .

Where does your heart line end?

INSTRUCTIONS: Your heart line should travel from someplace near your index finger toward the other side of your hand. Heart lines end in different places on everybody's hands.

HINT: Follow your heart line to the end.

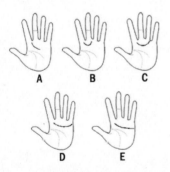

A. middle of the hand (go to page 170)
B. below the middle finger (go to page 171)
C. below the ring finger (go to page 172)
D. below the pinky finger (go to page 173)
E. other side of the palm (go to page 174)

Red hot!
Your red heart line is a sign of unbridled passion and extreme desires. This is no surprise for a Venusian like yourself. You are overwhelmed with emotion and you have a difficult time keeping your feelings to yourself.

You may want to slow down. Too much of anything can be dangerous and in this case you may end up scaring away some terrific opportunities for romance.

Let's continue your reading. . .

Do you have any lines on the side of your hand below your pinky?

INSTRUCTIONS: If you make a loose fist and look at the side of your hand between your pinky finger and your heart line you may notice some lines. These lines of affection are usually easily found, but on some rare occasions they may be completely missing.

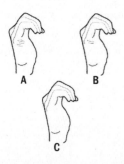

HINT: Make a fist and examine the side of your hand.

A. three or more (go to page 167)
B. one or two (go to page 168)
C. none (go to page 169)

A yellow heart?

Your yellow heart line may be a sign of trouble. You may just be turned off by romance and everything it entails. You appear to be content with solitude and your individual needs.

At this moment the idea of providing for anyone else is very unappealing for you. You aren't selfish, you're just not sure if you're ready for romance. The single life may be best for you right now.

Let's continue your reading. . .

Where does your heart line end?

INSTRUCTIONS: Your heart line should travel from someplace near your index finger toward the other side of your hand. Heart lines end in different places on everybody's hands.

HINT: Follow your heart line to the end.

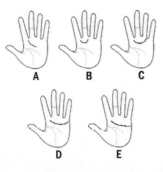

A. middle of the hand (go to page 170)
B. below the middle finger (go to page 171)
C. below the ring finger (go to page 172)
D. below the pinky finger (go to page 173)
E. other side of the palm (go to page 174)

A heart with the blues

Your blue heart line indicates that you may be struggling with your love life. You're having a difficult time making decisions. You are confused.

It's healthy to think things through, but you may be thinking a bit too much. The stress may begin to overwhelm you and your personal health may suffer. Relax and go with your feelings. Don't be afraid to make a mistake.

Let's continue your reading. . .

Do you have any lines on the side of your hand below your pinky?

INSTRUCTIONS: If you make a loose fist and look at the side of your hand between your pinky finger and your heart line you may notice some lines. These lines of affection are usually easily found, but on some rare occasions they may be completely missing.

HINT: Make a fist and examine the side of your hand.

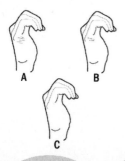

A. three or more (go to page 167)
B. one or two (go to page 168)
C. none (go to page 169)

A pale heart
You may have a heart line, but its pale coloring may leave you feeling cold and lonely. You are certain to have trouble finding love, and even when you've found it you may struggle to keep it.

Don't surrender to the symbols and signs found on your hand. You control your own destiny. If you are serious about improving your love life just make the extra effort. Over time you'll notice that your pale lines will turn to pink!

Let's continue your reading. . .

Which two fingers have the most space between them?

INSTRUCTIONS: Relax your hand and hold it in front of you. Hold your fingers out in their most natural and comfortable position. Now you can see if your fingers are spaced evenly.

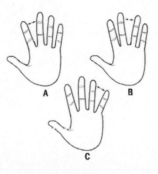

HINT: Be sure to relax your hand.

A. index finger and middle finger
   (go to page 130)
B. middle finger and ring finger
   (go to page 131)
C. ring finger and pinky finger
   (go to page 132)

Pretty in pink

Your pink heart line is a pleasant reward for being compassionate and warm. As long as your heart line retains this shading you are sure to be a true romantic.

You are unlikely to fall in love with someone who holds a pale heart line, but if you do it's certain that your affection will turn their heart line pink.

Let's continue your reading. . .

Which third of your hand is the most pronounced?

INSTRUCTIONS: Your hand is divided into three sections: the upper, middle, and lower. Use the image to assist you in determining which section of your hand is most pronounced. This isn't always easy to do. Answer to the best of your ability.

HINT: Decide which section of your hand dominates.

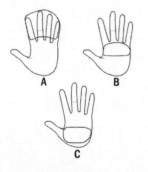

A. upper third (go to page 110)
B. middle third (go to page 111)
C. lower third (go to page 112)

Red hot!

Your red heart line is a sign of unbridled passion and extreme desires. You are overwhelmed with emotion and you have a difficult time keeping your feelings to yourself.

You may want to slow down. Too much of anything can be dangerous and in this case you may end up scaring away some terrific opportunities for romance.

Let's continue your reading. . .

Which two fingers have the most space between them?

INSTRUCTIONS: Relax your hand and hold it in front of you. Hold your fingers out in their most natural and comfortable position. Now you can see if your fingers are spaced evenly.

HINT: Be sure to relax your hand.

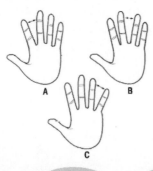

A. index finger and middle finger
(go to page 130)
B. middle finger and ring finger
(go to page 131)
C. ring finger and pinky finger
(go to page 132)

A yellow heart?
Your yellow heart line may be a sign of trouble. You may just be turned off by romance and everything it entails. You appear to be content with solitude and your individual needs.

At this moment the idea of providing for anyone else is very unappealing for you. You aren't selfish, you're just not sure if you're ready for romance. The single life may be best for you right now.

Let's continue your reading. . .

Which third of your hand is the most pronounced?
INSTRUCTIONS: Your hand is divided into three sections: the upper, middle, and lower. Use the image to assist you in determining which section of your hand is most pronounced. This isn't always easy to do. Answer to the best of your ability.

HINT: Decide which section of your hand dominates.

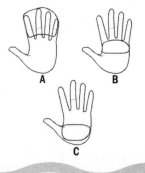

A. upper third (go to page 110)
B. middle third (go to page 111)
C. lower third (go to page 112)

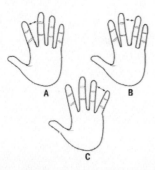

A heart with the blues

Your blue heart line indicates that you may be struggling with your love life. You're having a difficult time making decisions. You are confused.

It's healthy to think things through, but you may be thinking a bit too much. The stress may begin to overwhelm you and your personal health may suffer. Relax and go with your feelings. Don't be afraid to make a mistake.

Let's continue your reading. . .

Which two fingers have the most space between them?

INSTRUCTIONS: Relax your hand and hold it in front of you. Hold your fingers out in their most natural and comfortable position. Now you can see if your fingers are spaced evenly.

HINT: Be sure to relax your hand.

A. index finger and middle finger
   (go to page 130)
B. middle finger and ring finger
   (go to page 131)
C. ring finger and pinky finger
   (go to page 132)

A chained heart

The effect of the chained lines on your hand is the weak operation of the qualities of the line. If chains are seen on only part of a line, the weak, poor operation of the line will occur. The chains make it impossible for your current to flow freely and evenly through the line, creating a labored, strained, obstructed condition. If the chain appears on your heart line you may be more sentimental than those around you. You may also have a tendency to become nervous and uncomfortable in risky relationships.

Let's continue your reading. . .

Where does your heart line end?

INSTRUCTIONS: Your heart line should travel from someplace near your index finger toward the other side of your hand. Heart lines end in different places on everybody's hands.

HINT: Follow your heart line to the end.

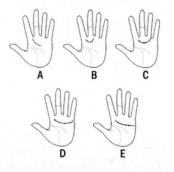

A. middle of the hand (go to page 182)
B. below middle finger (go to page 184)
C. below ring finger (go to page 186)
D. below pinky finger (go to page 188)
E. other side of the palm (go to page 190)

Islands of the heart

The island formation on the lines of your hand divides the strength of the current, producing a consequent division of strength and force thus lessening their vital force. If you find significant islands on your heart line you will face some challenging times in your love life.

Let's continue your reading. . .

Where does your heart line end?

INSTRUCTIONS: Your heart line should travel from someplace near your index finger toward the other side of your hand. Heart lines end in different places on everybody's hands.

HINT: Follow your heart line to the end.

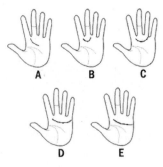

A. middle of the hand (go to page 182)
B. below middle finger (go to page 184)
C. below ring finger (go to page 186)
D. below pinky finger (go to page 188)
E. other side of the palm (go to page 190)

A *crossed heart*

The crossed lines that appear on your hands are a common sign. A deep-cut cross is a sign of grave importance, especially if highly colored. The cross is an obstacle or a defect, and can produce a bad quality or a change in the course of your love life. Imagine the current of love running through your heart line. When your heart line crosses another line the strength of the line is diminished. Subsequently your heart line reflects a dwindling passion.

Let's continue your reading. . .

Where does your heart line end?

INSTRUCTIONS: Your heart line should travel from someplace near your index finger toward the other side of your hand. Heart lines end in different places on everybody's hands.

HINT: Follow your heart line to the end.

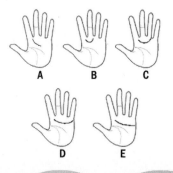

A. middle of the hand (go to page 182)
B. below middle finger (go to page 184)
C. below ring finger (go to page 186)
D. below pinky finger (go to page 188)
E. other side of the palm (go to page 190)

A broken heart line

The breaks in the lines on your hand are frequently encountered and often indicate a defective condition. It signifies that the current is interrupted and stopped in exactly the same manner as when a telephone wire is cut. In some cases, the lines may eventually grow together or the current may jump over the break.

The wider the break, the more serious it becomes and the less likelihood there is of the current's passing over the space between the broken ends. The effects of this may be felt in your love life if the breaks are on the heart line and your head line.

Where does your heart line end?

INSTRUCTIONS: Your heart line should travel from someplace near your index finger toward the other side of your hand. Heart lines end in different places on everybody's hands.

HINT: Follow your heart line to the end.

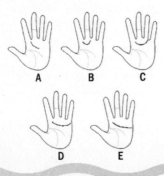

A. middle of the hand (go to page 182)
B. below middle finger (go to page 184)
C. below ring finger (go to page 186)
D. below pinky finger (go to page 188)
E. other side of the palm (go to page 190)

Your heart runs into your head

You have indicated that your heart line intersects your head line. This is a troubling discovery, as it reflects your inability to maintain stability in your relationships. Subsequently, you might have a tendency to overanalyze your relationships and this may ultimately lead you to have trouble finding a long-lasting romance. You may want to take more time to step back and enjoy the little things. Try not to overanalyze the romantic behavior of your lover.

Which third of your hand is the most pronounced?

INSTRUCTIONS: Your hand is divided into three sections: the upper, middle, and lower. Use the image to assist you in determining which section of your hand is most pronounced. This isn't always easy to do. Answer to the best of your ability.

HINT: Decide which section of your hand dominates.

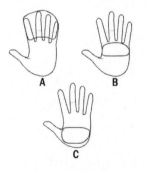

A. upper third (go to page 110)
B. middle third (go to page 111)
C. lower third (go to page 112)

A fickle heart

You have indicated that your heart line intersects both your head line and your life line. This is a very unsettling discovery. This indicates that you are exceedingly irritable, changeable in affections, constantly seeking excitement, and difficult to get along with.

Your relationships will suffer if your attitude fails to change. Don't let this discovery influence you. You need to make the best of the situation.

Which third of your hand is the most pronounced?

INSTRUCTIONS: Your hand is divided into three sections: the upper, middle, and lower. Use the image to assist you in determining which section of your hand is most pronounced. This isn't always easy to do. Answer to the best of your ability.

HINT: Decide which section of your hand dominates.

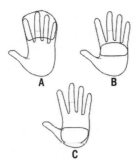

A. upper third (go to page 110)
B. middle third (go to page 111)
C. lower third (go to page 112)

Level headed

It's nice to see that your heart line does not appear to intersect with your head line or life line. Keep in mind this could change with time. If your heart line begins to migrate to your head line it will be a reflection of possible turmoil in your relationships.

Keep a close eye on your heart line, in particular when you have entered into new relationships. Your heart line's behavior can change in just a matter of months.

Now let's continue with your reading. . .

Which third of your hand is the most pronounced?

INSTRUCTIONS: Your hand is divided into three sections: the upper, middle, and lower. Use the image to assist you in determining which section of your hand is most pronounced. This isn't always easy to do. Answer to the best of your ability.

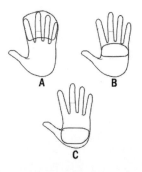

HINT: Decide which section of your hand dominates.

A. upper third (go to page 110)
B. middle third (go to page 111)
C. lower third (go to page 112)

You have just completed your personalized love reading. Now that you've revealed the secrets in the palm of your hand, it's time for you to take a look at the palms of those around you. Whether it's a boyfriend, girlfriend, or best friend, palm reading can provide you with valuable insight related to the world of romance. Remember your hand changes over time so be sure to refer to this book whenever you come to a fork in the road. See you soon!